Recommendations of Kothari Commission

Recommendations of Kothari Commission

Dr. R.K. Raghuram

CRESCENT
PUBLISHING CORPORATION

[The responsibility for the facts stated, conclusions reached and plagiarism, if any, in this book is entirely that of the Author. And the Publisher bears no responsibility for them, whatsoever.]

Recommendations of Kothari Commission

First Published : 2016

ISBN 978-81-8342-149-2

Published by :
CRESCENT PUBLISHING CORPORATION
4831/24, Prahlad Street,
Ansari Road, Darya Ganj,
New Delhi - 110002
Ph. : 23272541, 23257835
Fax : 91- 011- 23257835
e-mail : campusbooks@hotmail.com

Printed at :
Roshan Offset Printers
Delhi

Preface

Considering the important role of education in the national development and in the building up of a truly democratic society, the Government of India considered it necessary to survey and examine the entire field of education in order to realise a well balanced, integrated and adequate system of national education capable of making a powerful contribution to all aspects of national life. To achieve these objectives speedily, in October 1964, the Government set up an Education Commission, under Resolution of July 14, 1964. The Commission in particular was to advise the government on the national pattern of education and on the general policies for the development of education at all stages—ranging from the primary to postgraduate stage and in all its aspects besides examining a host of educational problems in their social and economic context.

The Commission, under the chairmanship of Dr. D. S. Kothari, Chairman. University Grants Commission, consisted of sixteen members. The Commission had the benefit of discussion with and advice of a number of internationally known consultants in the educational as well as scientific field. From the very beginning the commission have been conscious of the immensity and inherent difficulties of the task assigned to us. The commission tried to bring, about major improvement in the effectiveness of primary education;

to introduce work experience as an integral element of general education; to vocationalise secondary education; to improve the quality of teachers at all levels and to provide teachers in sufficient strength; to liquidate illiteracy; to strengthen centres of advanced study and strive to attain, in some of our universities at least, higher international standards; to lay special emphasis on the combination of teaching and research; and to pay particular attention to education and research in agriculture and allied sciences.

The recommendations of Kothari Commission is a landmark in the history of Indian education. All recommendations calls for a determined and large-scale action. This book covers all aspects of commission's recommendations and views on education. It is hoped that the insight and comprehensive information of the book prompts readers into paying more attention to and action for effective educational development.

Dr. R.K. Raghuram

Contents

1

Introduction

The origin of the present system of education which is prevalent in this country today can be traced to the beginning of the nineteenth century when a controversy had been raging over the issue whether oriental learning and science should be spread through the medium of Sanskrit, Arabic or Persian or Western sciences and literature be spread through English as the medium of instruction. The Government conducted surveys of the then prevalent systems of education with a view to re-organising education to suit the needs of the times. Consequent on Macaulay's Minute regarding the educational policy of the future, Lord William Bentick's Government issued a communique wherein it was stated " that the great object of the British Government ought to be the promotion of European literature and science among the natives of India; and that all the funds appropriated for the purpose of education alone". The Government Resolution, however, stated that provision should be made for the continuance of schools and colleges where indigenous learning was being imparted.

Early Educational Commissions

By 1853 a number of problems concerning education in the country had risen which required immediate solution. As a result of an inquiry made by the Government, Sir

Charles Wood, the then Secretary of state, sent a despatch popularly known as Wood's Despatch to the Court of the Directors of the East India Company in 1854. The despatch enunciated the aim of education as the diffusion of the Arts, Science, Philosophy and Literature of Europe. It laid down that the study of Indian languages was to be encouraged and that the English language should be taught wherever there was a demand for it, and that both English and the Indian Languages were to be regarded the media for the diffusion of European knowledge; a scheme to establish universities was to be formulated, whose functions were to hold examinations and corder degrees. The despatch also recommended that a number of high schools should-be set up4. This eventually led to the establishment in the country of the first three universities in 1857.

In 1882 the Government of India appointed a Commission, known as the Hunter Commission, "to enquire into the manner in which, effect had been given to the principles of the Despatch of 1854 and to suggest such measures as it may think desirable in order to further carrying out of the policy therein laid down". The Commission, inter alia, recommended the gradual withdrawal of the State from the direct support and management of institutions of higher education. With regard to vocational and technical education, the Commission recommended that in the particular class of high schools there should be two avenues, one leading to the entrance examination of the University and the other of a more practical character intended to fit the youth for commercial, vocational and non-literary pursuits.

The recommendations of the Hunter Commission led to a rapid expansion of higher education during the next two decades, giving rise to problems which necessitated the appointment of a Commission on January 27, 1902, "to enquire into the condition and prospects of the universities established in British India; to consider and report upon any proposals which have been, or may be made for improving their constitution and working, and to recommend such measures as may tend to elevate the standard of university teaching, and to promote the advancement of learning". The Commission recommended the reorganisation of university administration; a much more strict and systematic supervision of the colleges by the university; and the imposition of more exacting conditions of affiliation; a much closer attention to the conditions under which students live and work; the assumption of teaching functions by the university within defined limits; substantial changes in curricula and in the methods of examination. As a result of the recommendations of this Commission secondary schools came to be more under the domination of the Universities: under the Indian Universities Act of 1904, schools had to be recognised by the Universities, and rules and regulations were framed for this purpose.

There was a growing popular demand in the country for mass education. A Government Resoultion on education policy was issued in 1913, enunciating three cardinal principles:

(i) that the standard of existing institutions should be raised in preference to increasing their number;

(ii) that the scheme of primary and secondary education for the average scholar should be steadily diverted to more practical ends; and

(iii) that-provision should be made for higher studies and research in India, so that Indian students might get enough facilities for higher work without having to go. abroad.

Though the Resolution was immediately carried into effect, the out break of the World War I delayed the developments planned in the Resolution. However, some new universities were established.

The next important stage was the appointment of the Calcutta University Commission in 1917 under the Chairmanship of the late Sir Michael Sadler. This Commission went into the question of secondary education and held the view that the improvement of secondary education was essential for the improvement of University education. The Commission made the following important recommendations:

(i) The dividing line between the University and Secondary courses should properly be drawn at the Intermediate examination than at the Matriculation Examination.

(ii) The Government should, therefore, create a new type of institution called the intermediate colleges which would provide for instruction in Arts, Science, Medicine, Engineering and Teaching etc; these colleges were to be run as independent institutions or to be attached to selected high schools.

(iii) The admission test' for universities should be the passing of the Intermediate examination.

(iv) A Board of Secondary and Intermediate Education, consisting of the representatives of Government, University, High Schools and Intermediate Colleges be established and entrusted with the administration and control of Secondary Education.

The Sadler Commission Report was a comprehensive one and many of the universities in India implemented its suggestions. It was also for the first time that a Commission had recommended the attachment of Intermediate Classes to the high schools and the setting up of a Board of Education to control High School and Intermediate Education.

In 1929, an Auxiliary Committee of the Indian Statutory Commission, known as the Hartog Committee after its Chairman Sir Philip Hartog was appointed to review the position of education in the country. In the opinion of this Committee. the Matriculation of the University still dominated the whole of the secondary course. In order to obviate this defect, the Committee recommended that a large number of pupils intending to follow certain avocation should stop at the middle school stage and there should be "more diversified curricula in the schools". The Committee also recommended diversion of more boys to industrial and commercial careers at the end of the middle stage, preparatory to special instruction in technical and industrial schools". The Committee also reviewed the problems relating to the training of teachers and the service conditions of the secondary teachers".

The Sapru Committee appointed in 1934 by the U.P. Government to enquire into the causes of unemployment in U.P. came to the conclusion that the system of education commonly prevalent prepared pubils only for examinations and degrees and not for any avocation in life. The Committee suggested that

(i) diversified courses at the secondary stage should be introduced, one of these leading to the University degree;'

(ii) the intermediate stage be abolished and the secondary stage be extended by one year;

(iii) the vocational training and education should begin after the lower secondary stage; and

(iv) the Degree course at the University should extend over a period of three years

In prusuance of the Resolution of 1935 of the Central-Advisory Board of Education, two expert advisers, Messrs. Abbot and Wood were invited in 1936 to advise the Government "on certain problems of educational reorganisation and particularly on problems of vocational education". The Abbot-Wood Report, submitted in 1937, suggested a complete hierarchy of vocational institutions parallel with the hierarchy of institutions imparting general education. As a result of their recommendations "a new type of technical institution called the Polytechnic has come into existence". The provinces also started technical, commercial or agricultural high-schools conducting non-literary courses

In 1937, the Congress Ministry assumed responsibility of administration in seven major Provinces of India and concentrated their attention on educational reforms. In October 1937, an all-India National Educational Conference was summoned at Wardha under the presidentship of Mahatma Gandhi and the following resolutions were adopted:

1. That in the opinion of this conference free and compulsory education be provided for seven years on a nation-wide scale;
2. That the medium of instruction be the mothertongue;
3. That the conference endorses the proposal made by Mahatma Gandhi that the process of education throughout this period should centre around some form of manual and productive work, and that all other abilities to be developed or training to be given should, as far as possible, be integrally related to the central handicraft chosen with due regard to the environment of the child; and
4. That the conference expects that this system of education will be gradually able to cover the remuneration of teachers.

The conference then appointed a committee with Dr. Zakir Hussain as its chairman. The Committee submitted its report on December 2, 1937, and the scheme of education suggested by it is popularly known as the "Wardha Scheme", the main features of which are as follows:

(i) A Basic Craft is to serve as the centre of instruction. The idea is not to teach some handicraft side by side with liberal education, but the entire education is to be imparted through some industry or vocation;

(ii) The scheme is to be self-supporting to the extent of covering teachers' salaries and aims at makng pupils self-supporting after the completion of their course;

(iii) Manual labour is insisted on so that every individual may learn to earn his living through it in liter life. It is also considered non-violent, since an individual does not snatch away the living of others with the help of a machine; and

(iv) Instruction is closely coordinated with the child's life, i.e., his home and village crafts and occupations.",

In 1944, the Central Advisory Board of Education submitted a comprehensive Report on Post-War Educational Development, known as the Sargent Report, visualising a system of universal, compulsory and free education for all boys and girls between the ages of 6 and 14, the Senior Basic or the Middle School to be the final stage in the school career of majority of the pupils. The Report also recommended that at the Middle School stage, provision should be made for a variety of courses, extending over a period of five years after the age of 11. These courses while preserving an essentially cultural character should be designed to prepare the pupils for entry into industrial and commercial occupations as well as into the Universities. It was recommended that the High School course should cover 6 years, the normal age of admission being 11 years and that the High Schools should be of two main types (a) academic, and (b) technical. The objective of both should be to provide a good all-round education combined with some preparation in the later stages for the careers which pupils will pursue on leaving schools.

The era of educational reconstruction inevitably followed in the wake of social and economic reconstruction initiated by the National Government after 1947, education being the chief instrument for reconstruction and transformation of society. The first steps taken in the direction of educational reconstruction were the appointment of a series of commissions to survey, study, review and recommend improvements in the different sectors of education.

To look into the problems of University education, the University Education Commission was appointed by the Government of India in 1948 under the Chairmanship of Dr. S. Radhakrishnan in pursuance of the recommendations of the Central Advisory Board of Education and also of the Inter-University Board. The Commission made important suggestions for improving the standard of university education in the country. Introduction of a three-year degree course for the first university degree, greater use of tutorial system of instruction, formulation of new aims, emphasis on developing knowledge and critical thinking rather than mechanical passing of examinations, establishment of Rural Universities and introduction of moral education were some of its salient recommendations. The Commission, however, thought it unfortunate that neither the public nor the Government had realised the importance of Intermediate Colleges in the Indian educational systems. To coordinate University Education in the country, the establishment of the University Grants Commission was also recommeided. The Commission came into being immediately there after.

The Radhakrishnan Commission had surveyed the field of secondary education in a passing manner and had admitted that 'our secondary education remains the weakest link in our educational machinery and needs urgent reform'. This fact was the raison d'etre of an All

India Commission for Secondary Education appointed in 1952 under the Chairmanship of Dr. A. Lakshmanswamy Mudaliar. This Commission offered a numbers of suggestions to adjust secondary education with the new goals and needs of free India. The aim was now to train our youth for intermediate leadership and for democratic citizenship. Secondary education was to be a terminal stage for a large majority of the nation's youth, who would take up their places in society after their school education and provide leadership to the general masses. The Commission was equally concerned with qualitative improvement of the schools. To develop individual talent, curricular offerings were extended and diversified. To achieve the new aims of education, changes in methods of teaching were suggested. New trends in examination, guidance and extra curricular work were brought into the school programmes. Multipurpose secondary school was a new concept recommended by the Commission. Inclusion of craft, social studies and general science in the curriculum was aimed at orienting students towards an industrial and science-centred democratic life.

Creation of Kothari Commission

In view of the important rote of education in the national development and in building up a truly democratic society the Government considered it necessary to survey and examine the entire field of education in order to realise a well balanced, integrated and adequate system of national education capable of making a powerful contribution to all aspects of national life. To achieve these objectives speedily, the Government of India in October 1964, set up an Education Commission, under Resolution of July 14, 1964.

The Commission in particular was to advise the Government on the national pattern of education and on the general policies for the Development of education at all stages-ranging from the primary to post-graduate stage and in all its aspects besides examining a host of educational problems in their social and economic context. The Commission was, however, not to examine legal and medical education.

The Commission, under the chairmanship of Dr. D. S. Kothari, Chairman. University Grants Commission, consisted of sixteen members. eleven being Indians and five foreign experts. In addition, the Commission had the benefit of discussion with and advice of a number of internationally known consultants in the educational as well as scientific field.

The Commission began its task twenty-one months ago, on October 2, 1964, Mahatma Gandhi's birthday. From the very beginning the commission have been conscious of the immensity and inherent difficulties of the task assigned to us. No task in the commission's view could be more challenging, more vital and relevant to India's progress and development-economic, cultural and spiritual.

In facing a task of such colossal magnitude and complexity, there is always a danger that the approach and recommendations may not be sufficiently radical. There is also the other possibility that the recommendations may go beyond the capacity and resources of the nation. The difficulties are greatly accentuated because educational plans are long-term plans, and long-term projections of needs and resources are beset with serious uncertainties.

Indian education needs a drastic reconstruction, almost a revolution. The commission tried to bring, about major improvement in the effectiveness of primary education; to introduce work experience as an integral element of general education; to vocationalize secondary education; to improve the quality of teachers at all levels and to provide teachers in sufficient strength; to liquidate illiteracy; to strengthen centres of advanced study and strive to attain, in some of our universities at least, higher international standards; to lay special emphasis on the combination of teaching and research; and to pay particular attention to education and research in agriculture and allied sciences. All this calls for a determined and large-scale action. Tinkering with the existing situation and moving forward with faltering steps and lack of faith can make things worse than before.

The Commission set up twelve Task Forces on

(1) School Education;

(2) Higher Education;

(3) Technical Education;

(4) Agricultural Education;

(5) Adult Education;

(6) Science Education and Research;

(7) Teacher Training and Teacher Status;

(8) Student Welfare;

(9) New Techniques and Methods;

(10) Manpower;

(11) Educational Administration; and

(12) Educational Finance.

In addition, it set up seven Working Groups on

(1) Women's Education;

(2) Education of Backward Classes;

(3) School Buildings;

(4) School-Community Relations;

(5) Statistics;

(6) Pre-Primary Education; and

(7) School Curriculum.

The Task Forces and the Working Groups made a detailed study of many specific problems. Some of these studies will be published separately. The Reports of the Task Forces and the Working Groups have been of great help to us in the commission's work and have enabled us to examine some of the important issues in a depth and detail which would not have been possible otherwise.

The commission members spent about one hundred days in going round all the States and some Union Territories. They visited universities, Colleges and schools and held discussions with teachers, educationists, administrators and students. They convened two conferences of university students' representatives to have the advantage of personal discussion with them about student welfare and discipline. They found these conferences of real value.

The commission interviewed men and women distinguished in public life, scientists, industrialists and scholars in different fields and others interested in education. Altogether the commission interviewed about 9,000 persons. The commission invited written evidence, memoranda and replies to the commission's questionnaires, organized seminars and conferences, commissioned a number of special studies and also conducted a few special enquiries such as the socioeconomic background of students admitted to educational institutions, and working days in schools and colleges. The total number of memoranda and notes sent to the Commission was over 2,400.

The commission had the benefit of valuable consultations with a number of internationally well-known educationists and scientists.

2

National Policy on Education, 1968

The Resolution issued by the Government of India on the Report of the Education Commission is reproduced below for ready reference.

Education has always been accorded an honoured place in Indian society. The great leaders of the Indian freedom movement realized the fundamental role of education and throughout the nation's struggle for independence, stressed its unique significance for national development. Gandhiji formulated the scheme of Basic Education seeking to harmonize intellectual and manual work. This was a great step forward in making education directly relevant to the life of the people. Many other national leaders likewise made important contributions to national education before independence.

In the post- Independence period, a major concern of the Government of India and of the States has been to give increasing attention to education as a factor vital to national progress and security. Problems of educational reconstruction were reviewed by several commissions and committees, notably the University Education Commission (1948-49) and the Secondary Education Commission (1952-53). Some steps to implement the recommendations of these Commissions were taken; and with the passing of the Resolution on Scientific Policy under the leadership of Jawaharlal Nehru, the development of science, technology and scientific research received special emphasis. Towards the end of the Third Five Year Plan, a need was felt to hold a comprehensive review of the educational system with a view to initiating a fresh and more determined effort at educational reconstruction; and the Education Commission (1964-66) was appointed to advise the Government on the national pattern of education and on the general principles and policies for the development of education at all stages and in all aspects". The Report of the Education Commission has since been widely discussed and commented upon. The Government is happy to note that a general consensus on the national policy on education has emerged in the course of these discussions.

The Government of India is convinced that a radical reconstruction of education on the broad lines recommended by the Education Commission is essential for economic and cultural development of the country, for national integration and for realizing the ideal of a socialistic pattern of society. This will involve a transformation of the system to relate it more closely to the life of the people; a continuous effort to expand educational opportunity; a sustained and intensive effort to raise the quality of education at all stages; an emphasis on the development of science and technology; and the cultivation of moral and social values. The educational system must produce young men and women of character and ability committed to national service and development. Only then will education be able to play its vital role in promoting national progress, creating a sense of common citizenship and culture, and strengthening national integration. This is necessary if the country is to attain its rightful place in the comity of nations in conformity with its great cultural heritage and its unique potentialities.

The Government of India accordingly resolves to promote the development of education in the country in accordance with the following principles:

(1) *Free and Compulsory Education.* Strenuous efforts should be made for the early fulfilment of the Directive Principle under Article 45 of the Constitution seeking to provide free and compulsory education for all children up to the age of 14. Suitable programmes should be developed to reduce the prevailing wastage and stagnation in schools and to ensure that every child who is enrolled in school successfully completes the prescribed course.

(2) *Status, Emoluments and Education of Teachers.*

(a) Of all factors which determine the quality of education and its contribution to national develop-ment, the teacher is Undoubtedly the most impor-tant. It is on his personal qualities and character, his educational qualifications and professional competence that the success of all educational endeavour must ultimately depend. Teachers must, therefore, be accorded an honoured place in society. Their emoluments and other service conditions should be adequate and satisfactory, having regard to their qualifications and responsibilities.

(b) The academic freedom of teachers to pursue and publish independent studies and researches and to speak and write about significant national and international issues should be protected.

(c) Teacher education, particularly in-service education, should receive due emphasis.

(3) *Development of Languages.*

(a) *Regional Languages*: The energetic development of Indian languages and literature is a sine qua non for educational and cultural development. Unless this is done, the creative energies of the people will not be released, standards of education will not improve, knowledge will not spread to the people, and the gulf between the intelligentsia and the masses will remain, if not widen further. The regional languages are already in use as media of education at the primary and secondary stages. Urgent steps should now be taken to adopt them as media of education at the university stage.

(b) *Three-Language Formula*: At the secondary stage, the State Governments should adopt, and vigorously implement, the three-language formula which 'includes the study of a modern Indian language, preferably one of the southern languages, apart from Hindi and English in the Hindi-speaking States, and of Hindi along with the regional language and English in the non-Hindi speaking States. Suitable courses in Hindi and/or English should also be available in universities and colleges with a view to improving the proficiency of students in these languages up to the prescribed university standards.

(c) *Hindi:* Every effort should be made to promote the development of Hindi. In developing Hindi as the link language, due care should be taken to ensure that it will serve, as provided for in Article 351 of the Constitution, as a medium of expression for all the elements of the composite culture of India. The establishment, in non-Hindi. States, of colleges and other institutions of higher education which use Hindi as the medium of education should be encouraged.

(d) *Sanskrit*: Considering the special importance of Sanskrit to the growth and development of Indian languages and its unique contribution to the cultural unity of the country, facilities for its teaching at the school and university stages should be offered on a more liberal scale. Development of new methods of teaching the language should be encouraged, and the possibility explored of including the study of Sanskrit in those courses (such as modern Indian languages, ancient Indian history, Indology and Indian philosophy) at the first and second degree stages, where such knowledge is useful.

(e) *International Languages:* Special emphasis needs to be laid on the study of English and other international languages. World knowledge is growing at a tremendous pace, especially in science and technology. India must not only keep up this growth but should also make her own significant contribution to it. For this purpose, study of English deserves to be specially strengthened.

(4) *Equalization of Educational Opportunity.* Strenuous efforts should be made to equalize educational opportunity.

(a) Regional imbalances in the provision of educational facilities should be corrected and good educational facilities should be provided in rural and other backward areas.

(b) To promote social cohesion and national integration the Common School System as recommended by the Education Commission should be adopted. Efforts should be made to improve the standard of education in general schools. All special schools like Public Schools should be required to admit students on the basis of merit and also to provide a prescribed proportion of free-studentships to prevent segregation of social classes. This will not, however, affect the rights of minorities under Article 30 of the Constitution.

(c) The education of girls should receive emphasis, not only on grounds of social justice, but also because it accelerates social transformation.

(d) More intensive efforts are needed to develop education among the backward classes and especially among the tribal people.

(e) Educational facilities for the physically and mentally handicapped children should be expanded and attempts should be made to develop integrated programmes enabling the handicapped children to study in regular schools.

(5) *Identification of Talent.* For the cultivation of excellence, it is necessary that talent in diverse fields should be identified at as early an age as possible, and every stimulus and opportunity given for its full development.

(6) *Work-experience and National Service.* The school and the community should be brought closer through suitable programmes of mutual service and support. Work-experience and national service, including participation in meaningful and challenging programmes of community service and national reconstruction, should accordingly become an integral part of education. Emphasis in these programmes should be on self-help, character formation and on developing a sense of social commitment.

(7) *Science Education and Research.* With a view to accelerating the growth of the national economy, science education and research should receive high priority. Science and mathematics should be an integral part of general education till the end of the school stage.

(8) *Education for Agriculture and Industry.* Special emphasis should be placed on the development of education for agriculture and industry.

(a) There should be at least one agricultural university in every State. These should, as far as possible, be single campus universities; but where necessary, they may have constituent colleges on different campuses. Other universities may also be assisted, where the necessary potential exists, to develop strong departments for the study of one or more aspects of agriculture.

(b) In technical education, practical training in industry should form an integral part of such education. Technical education and research should be related closely to industry, encouraging the flow of personnel both ways and providing for continuous cooperation in the provision, design and periodical review of training programmes and facilities.

(c) There should be a continuous review of the agricultural, industrial and other technical manpower needs of the country and efforts should be made continuously to maintain a proper balance between the output of the educational institutions and employment opportunities.

(9) *Production of Books.* The quality of books should be improved by attracting the best writing talent

through a liberal policy of incentives and remuneration. Immediate steps should be taken for the production of high quality textbooks for schools and universities. Frequent changes of textbooks should be avoided and their prices should be low enough for students of ordinary means to buy them.

The possibility of establishing autonomous book corporations oil commercial lines should be examined and efforts should be made to have a few basic textbooks common throughout the country. Special attention should be given to books for children and to universitylevel books in regional languages.

(10) *Examinations.* A major goal of examination reforms should be to improve the reliability and validity of examinations and to make evaluation a continuous process aimed at helping the student to improve his level of achievement rather than at 'certifying' the quality of his performance at a given moment of time.

(11) *Secondary Education.*

(a) Educational opportunity at the secondary (and higher) level is a major instrument of social change and transformation. Facilities for secondary education should accordingly be extended expeditiously to the areas and classes which have been denied these in the past.

(b) There is a need to increase facilities for technical and vocational education at this stage. Provision of facilities for secondary and vocational education should conform broadly to the requirements of the developing economy and real employment opportunities. Such linkage is necessary to make technical and vocational education at the secondary stage effectively terminal. Facilities for technical and vocational education should be suitably diversified to cover a large number of fields, such as agriculture, industry, trade and commerce, medicine and public health, home management, arts and crafts, secretarial training, etc.

(12) *University Education*

(a) The number of wholetime students to be admitted to a college or university department should be determined with reference to the laboratory, library and other facilities and to the strength of the staff.

(b) Considerable care is needed in establishing new universities. These should be started only after an adequate provision of funds has been made for the purpose and due care has been taken to ensure proper standards.

(c) Special attention should be given to the organization of postgraduate courses and to the improvement of standards of training and research at this level.

(d) Centres of advanced study should be strengthened and a small number of 'clusters of centres' aiming at the highest possible standards in research and training should be established.

(e) There is a need to give increased support to research in universities generally. The institutions for research should, as far as possible, function within the fold of universities or in intimate association with them.

(13) *Part-time Education and Correspondence Courses.* Part-time education and correspondence courses should be developed on a large scale at the university stage. Such facilities should also be developed for

secondary school students, for teachers and for agricultural, industrial and other workers. Education through part-time and correspondence courses should be given the same status as full-time education. Such facilities will smoothen transition from school to work, promote the cause of education and provide opportunities to the large number of people who have the desire to educate themselves further but cannot do so on a full-time basis.

(14) *Spread of Literacy and Adult Education*

(a) The liquidation of mass illiteracy is necessary not only for promoting participation in the working of democratic institutions and for accelerating programmes of production, especially in agriculture, but for quickening the tempo of national development in general. Employees in large commercial, industrial and other concerns should come from the industrial undertakings in the public sector. Teachers and students should be actively involved in organizing literacy campaigns, especially as part of the social and National Service Programme.

(b) Special emphasis should be given to the education of young practising farmers and to the training of youth for selfemployment.

(15) *Games and Sports.* Games and sports should be developed on a large scale with the object of improving the physical fitness and sportsmanship of the average student as well as of those who excel in this department. Where playing field and other facilities for developing a nation-wide programme of physical education do not exist, these should be provided on a priority basis.

(16) *Education of Minorities.* Games and sports should be made not only to protect the rights of minorities but

to promote their educational interests as suggested in the statement issued by the conference of the Chief Ministers of States and Central ministers held in August 1961.

(17) *The Educational Structure.* It will be advantageous to have a broadly uniform educational structure in all parts of the country. The ultimate objective should be to adopt the 10+2+3 pattern, the higher secondary stage of two years being located in schools, colleges or both according to local conditions.

The reconstruction of education on the lines indicated above will need additional outlay. The aim should be gradually to increase the investment in education so as to reach a level of expenditure of 6percent of the national income as early as possible.

The Government of India recognizes that reconstruction of education is no easy task. Not only are the resources scare but the problems are exceedingly complex. Considering the key role which education, science and research play in developing the material and human resources of the country, the Government of India will, in addition to undertaking programmes in the Central sector, assist the State Governments for the development of programmes of national importance where coordinated action on the part of the States and the Centre is called for.

The Government of India will also review, every five years, the progress made and recommend guidelines for future development.

3

Educational Objectives

The destiny of India is now being shaped in her classrooms. This is no mere rhetoric. In a world based on science and technology it is education that determines the level of prosperity, welfare and security of the people. On the quality and number of persons coming out of our schools and colleges will depend our success in the great enterprise of national reconstruction the principal objective of which is to raise the standard of living of our people. in this context, it has become urgent:

— to re-evaluate the role of education in the total programme of national development;

— to identify the changes needed in the existing system of education if it is to play its proper role, and to prepare a programme of educational development based on them; and

— to implement this programme with determination and vigour.

The task is neither unique nor quite new. But its magnitude, gravity and urgency have increased immensely and it has acquired a new meaning and importance since the attainment of independence and the adoption of the policy and techniques of planned development of the national economy. If the pace of national development is to be accelerated, there is need for a well'-defined, bold and imaginative educational policy and for determined and vigorous action to vitalize, improve and expand education.

The population of India is now about 500 million, and half of it is below the age of 18 years-India today is essentially a land of youth. Over the next 20 years, the population is likely to increase by 230 million. The total number of educational institutions in the country is over 500,000. The number of teachers exceeds two million. The total student population, which is now about 70 million, will be more than doubled in the next twenty years; and by 1985, it will become about 170 million or about equal to the total population of Europe. The size and complexity of these problems argue the need for rapid action in evolving an appropriate educational policy; given this, the numbers involved constitute a rich promise for education's contribution to national development.

Education cannot be considered in isolation or planned in a vacuum. It has to be used as a powerful instrument of social, economic and political change and will therefore, have to be related to the long-term national aspirations, the programmes of national development on which the country is engaged and the difficult short-term problems it is called upon to face.

Problems of National Development

Self-sufficiency in Food

The first and the most important of these is food. Mahatma Gandhi said: 'If God were to appear in India, He will have to take the form of a loaf of bread'. Even at its present level of population, the country is in short supply for food. Every five years, the addition to the population is greater than the entire population of the

U.K. During the next two decades, there will be an addition of about 230 million persons (or 46 per cent of the population of 1966) even on the assumption that the existing birthrate of 40 per thousand persons is reduced to half by 1986. If it is not, this increase may be 320 million or 65 per cent of the present population. On the basis of present trends, in another 10-15 years, no country is likely to have a surplus of food to export. Even if such surpluses existed, we would have no resources to import the huge quantities of food required, or even to import the fertilizers needed. Self-sufficiency in food thus becomes not merely a desirable goal but a condition for survival.

Economic Growth and Full Employment

Allied to this is the colossal poverty of the masses and the large incidence of underemployment or unemployment among the people, particularly among the educated. India is one of the poorest countries of the world. The national income per capita, which was practically stationary for some decades, rose from Rs. 256.5 in 1950-51 to Rs. 348.6 in 1964-65-an increase of 2.2 per cent per year (at 1960-61 prices). Both the rate of growth as well as the level of national income are unsatisfactory. What is worse, even this income is very unevenly distributed. It has been suggested that our immediate objective should be to assure a minimum consumption of Rs. 35 per month to every citizen, sufficient to cover the balanced diet recommended by the Nutrition Advisory Committee and leave a modest allowance for other essential items (at 1960-61 prices). This, by itself, is no high standard. But at present, only the top 20 per cent of the population can afford it. The lowest 30 per cent have a monthly income of less than Rs. 15 and the lowest ten per cent, of less than Rs. 10. If this minimum standard of Rs. 35 per month is to be reached by 1986, great effort will have to be made on three fronts. The first is to secure a rapid rate of economic growth, at not less than six per cent per year and if possible at about seven percent per year. The second is to distribute income more equitably so that the more deprived sections of the population could have a comparatively larger share in the total national income. The third is to control the growth of population so that the birth-rate is reduced at least by one-third and preferably by half. The least to be attempted would be to double the national income per capita (at constant prices) in the next twenty years. Similarly, steps will have to be taken to provide full employment to the people, especially to the educated.

Social and National Integration

Even more important is the role of education in achieving social and national integration. Indian society is hierarchical, stratified and deficient in vertical mobility. The social distance between the different classes, particularly between the rich and the poor, the educated and the uneducated, is large and is tending to widen. Our people profess a number of different religions; and the picture becomes even more complicated because of caste, an undemocratic institution which is still powerful and which, strangely enough, seems to have extended its sphere of influence under the very democratic processes of the Constitution itself. The situation, complex as it was, has been made critical by recent developments which threaten both national unity and social progress. As education is not rooted in the traditions of the people, the educated persons tend to be alienated from their own culture. The growth of local, regional, linguistic and state loyalties tends to make the people forget 'India'. The old values, which held society together, are disappearing, and as there is no effective programme to replace them by a new sense of social responsibility, innumerable signs of social disorganization are. evident everywhere and are continually on the increase. These include strikes, increasing lawlessness and a disregard for public property, corruption in public life, and communal tensions and troubles. Student unrest, of which so much is written, is only one, and probably a minor one, of these symptoms. Against this background, the task to be attempted-the creation of an integrated and egalitarian society-is indeed extremely difficult and challenging.

Political Development

The political challenge has many aspects, but three stand out. The first is the need to strengthen democracy. In spite of all odds, Indian democracy has given a fairly good account of itself so far. But it will not be permanently viable unless its foundations are deepened by the creation of an educated electorate, and a dedicated and competent leadership, and the cultivation of essential values like self-control, tolerance, mutual goodwill and consideration for others, all of which make democracy not only a form of government, but a way of life. The second is related to the defence of the country's freedom. The overriding priority of this challenge is recognized, for one must live before one can grow. But it cannot be met only by maintaining a large and efficient army or training all able-bodied youth for military service. The defence of freedom is a national concern, to which every citizen contributes his best in order to achieve self-sufficiency in food and other essentials, to strengthen the country's economy, and to create a secular, united and strong democratic State. The third is the growing awakening among the masses who, suppressed for centuries, have now awakened to a sense of their rights and are demanding education, equality, higher standards of living and better civic amenities. This 'explosion of expectations' has also to be met through a planned programme of national development.

Internationally, the country is facing another equally significant and urgent challenge. The gap between the standards of living in India and those of industrialized nations is very large. The first scientific industrial revolution which developed in the West over the last 200 years almost passed us by. The agro-industrial revolution which is even more crucial for us has yet to begin in our country. The world is now at the beginning of the second scientific industrial revolution of automation and cybernetics, which is likely to be in full swing before the close of the century. It is difficult to visualize the changes it will make in man's life. One thing, however, is certain: unless proper steps are taken right from now, the gap between us and the industrialized countries following this second revolution may become too wide to be bridged.

There is still another aspect to the challenge. It is true that knowledge is international and that there can be no barriers, except those of our own creation, to its free import. But India cannot for ever remain at the receiving end of the pipeline. She must make her own contribution as an intellectual and cultural equal to the eternal human endeavour to extend the frontiers of knowledge. This demands a large-scale programme for the discovery and development of talent and the creation of centres of excellence in higher education which can compare favourably with the best of their kind in the world.

The difficulty of these problems is equalled only by the complexity of the situation, the gravity and urgency of the challenge, and the magnitude of the stakes involved. The Indian situation with its federal constitution, its multi-party system of democratic government, its multi-religious and mixed society consisting of highly sophisticated groups who live side by side with primitive ones, its mixed economy which includes modern factories as well as traditional agriculture, and its multiplicity of languages, presents such a complex picture that it almost resembles a miniature world.

In India's attempts at national development, the welfare of one-seventh of the world's population is at stake and the future of democracy and free societies is in the balance. She is heir to an ancient and great civilization which can make a contribution to human progress by striving to create what Acharya Vinobaji has described as the 'age of science and spirituality'. She has to raise herself from her present standards of living which are amongst the lowest in the world and to take her rightful place in the comity of nations as soon as possible-a task to be accomplished within a generation at the most. Obviously, the solution of these problems makes large demands on us, the Indian people of this generation—we need a clear focus, deeper understanding, collective discipline, hard and sustained work, and dedicated leadership. The solution of these problems also needs the cooperation and assistance of the richer industrialized nations which share India's faith in democratic socialism and sympathize with her struggle to create a new social order.

Education an Instrument of Change

These difficult, complex, significant and urgent problems are all interdependent, and the shortest and most effective way to their solution is obviously to make a simultaneous attack on all fronts. This will have to be attempted through two main programmes:

(1) The development of physical resources through the modernization of agriculture and rapid industrialization. This requires the adoption of a science-based technology, heavy capital formation and investment, and the provision of the essential

infrastructure of transport, credit, marketing and other institutions; and

(2) The development of human resources through a properly organized programme of education.

It is the latter programme, namely, the development of human resources through education, which is the more crucial of the two. While the development of physical resources is a means to an end, that of human resources is an end in itself; and without it, even the adequate development of physical resources is not possible.

The reason for this is clear. The realization of the country's aspirations involves changes in the knowledge, skills, interests and values of the people as a whole. This is basic to every programme of social and economic betterment of which India stands in need.

For instance, there can be no hope of making the country selfsufficient in food unless the farmer himself is moved out of his agelong conservatism through a science-based education, becomes interested in experimentation, and is ready to adopt techniques that increase yields. The same is true of industry. The skilled manpower needed for the relevant research and its systematic application to agriculture, industry and other sectors of life can only come from a development of scientific and technological education. Similarly, economic growth is not merely a matter of physical resources or of training skilled workers; it needs the education of the whole population in new ways of life, thought and work.

Robert Heilbroner describes the journey to economic development undertaken by a traditional society as 'the great ascent' and points out that the essential condition for its success is human 'change on a grand scale'. He observes: 'The mere lay-in of a core of capital equipment, indispensable as that is for further economic expansion, does not yet catalyse a tradition-bound society into a modern one. For that catalysis to take place, nothing short of a pervasive social transformation will suffice; a wholesale metamorphosis of habits, a wrenching reorientation of values concerning time, status, money, work; and an unweaving and reweaving of the fabric of daily existence itself.'

If this 'change, on a grand scale' is to be achieved without violent revolution there is one instrument, and one instrument only, that can be used: *Education*. Other agencies may help, and can indeed sometimes have a more apparent impact. But the national system of education is the only instrument that can reach all the people. It is not, however, a magic wand to wave wishes into existence. it is a difficult instrument, whose effective use requires strength of Will, dedicated work and sacrifice. But it is a sure and tried instrument, which has served other countries well in their struggle for development. It can, given the will and the skill, do so for India.

This emphasis on the social purposes of education, on the need to use it as a tool for the realization of national aspirations or for meeting national challenges, does not imply any underestimation of values for the individual. In a democracy, the individual is an end in himself and the primary purpose of education is to provide him with the widest opportunity to develop his potentialities to the full. But the path to this goal lies through social reorganization and emphasis on social perspectives. In fact, one of the important principles to be emphasized in the socialistic pattern of society, which the nation desires to create, is that individual fulfilment will come, not through selfish and narrow loyalties to personal or group interests, but through the dedication of all to the wider loyalties of national development in all its parameters.

Educational Revolution

This direct link between education, national development and prosperity which the Kothari commission have emphasized and in which it deeply believe, exists only when the national system of education is properly organized, both qualitatively and quantitatively. The naive belief that all education is necessarily good, both for the individual and for society, and that it will necessarily lead to progress, can be as harmful as it is misplaced. Quantitatively, education can be organized to promote social justice or to retard it. History shows numerous instances where small social groups and elites have used education as a prerogative of their rule and as a tool for maintaining their hegemony and perpetuating the values upon which it has rested. On the other hand, there are cases in which a social and cultural revolution has been brought about in a system where equality of educational opportunity is provided and education is deliberately used to develop more and more potential talent and to harness it to the solution of national problems. The same is even more true of the quality of education. A system of university education which produces a high proportion of competent professional manpower is of great assistance in increasing productivity and promoting economic growth. Another system of higher education with the same total output but producing a large proportion of indifferently educated graduates of arts, many of whom remain unemployed or are even unemployable, could create social tensions and retard economic growth. It is only the right type of education, provided on an adequate scale, that can lead to national development; when these conditions are not satisfied, the opposite effect may result.

The present system of education, designed to meet the needs of ail imperial administration within the limitations set by a feudal and traditional society, will need radical changes if it is to meet the purposes of a modem democratic and socialistic society-changes in objectives, in content, in teaching methods, in programmes, in the size and composition of the student body, in the selection and professional preparation of teachers, and in organization. In fact, what is needed is a revolution in education which in turn will set in motion the much desired social, economic and cultural revolution.

Existing System of Education

The existing system of education is largely unrelated to life and there is a wide gulf between its content and purposes and the concerns of national development. For instance,

— the educational system does not reflect the supreme importance of agriculture which is neglected at all stages and does not attract an adequate share of the top talent in the country; enrolment in the agricultural faculties of universities is extremely low; and agricultural colleges are comparatively weak and underdeveloped;

— the main task before the nation is to secure rapid economic development. If this is to be successfully accomplished, education must be related to productivity. The present system is too academic to be of material help in increasing national wealth;

— the schools and colleges are largely unconcerned with the great national effort at reconstruction and teachers and students generally remain uncommitted to it. They are often even unaware of its principles and very rarely have opportunities to participate ill its programmes;

— instead of promoting social and national integration and making an active effort to promote national consciousness, several features of the educational system promote divisive tendencies; caste loyalties are encouraged in a number of private educational institutions; the rich and the poor are segregated, the former attendIng the better type of private schools which charge fees while the latter are forced, by circumstances, to attend free government or local authority schools of poor quality; and

— at a time when the need to cultivate a sense of moral and social responsibility in the rising generation is paramount, education does not emphasize character-formation and makes little or no effort to cultivate moral and spiritual values, particularly the interests, attitudes and values needed for a democratic and socialistic society.

There is hardly any need to multiply such instances. The nature of the transformation needed in our educational system is generally recognized. Traditional societies which desire to modernize themselves have to transform their educational system before trying to expand it, because the greater the expansion of the traditional system of education, the more difficult and costly it becomes to change its character. This truth has been lost sight of and, during recent years, we have greatly expanded a system which continues to have essentially the same features it had at its creation about a century ago.

According to the Kothari Commision, therefore, no reform is more important or more urgent than to transform education, to endeavour to relate it to the life, needs and aspirations of the people and thereby make it a powerful instrument of social, economic and cultural transformation necessary for the realization of our national goals. This can be done if education is related to productivity;

— strengthens social and national integration; consolidates democracy as a form of government and helps the country to adopt it as a way of life;
— hastens the process of modernization; and
— strives to build character by cultivating social, moral and spiritual values.

All these aspects are interrelated and in the complex process of social change, we cannot achieve even one without striving for all.

EDUCATION AND PRODUCTIVITY

India is in transition from a society in which education is a privilege of a small minority to one in which it could be made available to the masses of the people. The immense resources needed for this programme can be generated only if education is related to productivity so that an expansion of education leads to an increase in national income which, in turn, may provide the means for a larger investment in education. Education and productivity call thus constitute a rising spiral' whose different parts sustain and support one another.

The link between education and productivity can be forged through the development of the following programmes which should receive high priority in the plans of educational reconstruction:

— making science a basic component of education and culture;
— making work-experience an integral part of general education;
— vocationalization of education, especially at the secondary school level, to meet the needs of industry, agriculture and trade; and

— improvement of scientific and technological education and research at the university stage with special emphasis on agriculture and allied sciences.

Science Education and Culture

A basic distinction between traditional and modem societies is the development and use by the latter of science-based technology which helps modernization of agriculture and the development of industries. In a traditional society, production is based largely on empirical processes, experience, and trial and error, rather than on science; in a modern society, it is basically rooted in science. The electrical industry was probably the first to become science-based; next came the chemical industry; and now, in industrialized countries, agriculture is fast becoming a branch of applied science. This close interlocking and interdependence between science and technology is a characteristic of the contemporary world. In recent years, several countries have been able to raise their GNP very rapidly because of their investment in basic science, technology and education.

Science strengthens the commitment of man to free enquiry and to the quest for truth as his highest duty and obligation. It loosens the bonds of dogmatism and acts as a powerful dispeller of fear and superstition, fatalism and passive resignation. By its emphasis on reason and free enquiry, it even helps to lessen ideological tensions which often arise because of adherence to dogma and fanaticism. Although it is largely occupied with the understanding of Nature at present, its development is tending more and more to help man to understand himself and his place ID the universe.

Work-experience

As another programme to relate education to life and productivity, the Kothari Commision recommend that work-experience should be introduced as an integral part of all education-general or vocational. The Commision define work-experience as participation in productive work in the school, in the home, in a workshop, on a farm, in a factory or in any other productive situation. According to the Commision, all good and purposeful education should consist of at least four basic elements:

— 'literacy' or a study of languages, the humanities and the social sciences;
— 'numeracy' or a study of mathematics and the natural sciences; work-experience; and
— social service.

In the present educational system, most of the time is taken up with the first, although even in this limited sphere, the attainments are not appreciable. The second, as indicated above, is still quite weak and needs a great deal of emphasis. But the third and fourth have been almost totally absent till recently and need to be highlighted-the former mainly for relating education to productivity, and the latter as a means of social and national integration.

The need to include work-experience as an integral part of education is to some extent inherent in the very nature and organization of formal education. Traditionally, an individual grew up in society through participation in its activities, and work-experience formed the bulk of his education. While this method had several advantages, its weakness consisted in that it was not essentially dynamic and forward-looking and tended to perpetuate traditional patterns of behaviour. Formal education, on the other hand, tended to withdraw the child temporarily from participation in community activities and to train him, in an artificial environment for his anticipated future role in society. This created a cleavage between the world of work and the world of study. This defect is particularly conspicuous in our system of education which tends to strengthen the tradition of denigrating work and alienates the students, particularly the first-generation learners, from their homes and communities. The introduction of workexperience is intended to overcome, to some extent, these weaknesses and to combine the advantages of the formal and informal systems of education.

Work-experience is thus a method of integrating education with work. This is not only possible but essential in modern societies which adopt science-based technology. In all traditional societies, an antithesis between education and work is usually postulated, partly because the techniques of production are primitive and do not necessarily require formal education, special skills or high intellectual ability, and partly because the work is generally manual, low-paid, akin to drudgery and confined mostly to the uneducated 'lower' classes.

As against this, education is generally the privilege of the upper classes who are interested, not in working for a living, but in the cultivation of interests which may help them in the enjoyment of life. The educated elite thus become largely parasitical in character and the real productive workers-at a low level of efficiency, generally-are the unlettered peasants and artisans. The complex techniques of production (including those in agriculture) adopted in modern societies, on the other hand, require higher forms of general or technical education and a comparatively higher level of intellectual ability.

High talent is required for research in technology, and even at the lower levels of work, brains become more important than physical strength. The traditional resistance of educated persons to engage themselves in productive work tends to disappear because, with the adoption of the new technology, work in industry or on the farm becomes more productive and remunerative and ceases to be looked down upon socially. The educated person thus becomes an important source of production and the uneducated person, an unproductive burden on society. This process, which has already started in our country, needs to be accelerated and therefore the inclusion of work-experience as an integral part of all education acquires an urgent significance.

The need to provide some such corrective to the overacademic nature of formal education has been widely recognized. In the curricula of most contemporary school systems, particularly in the socialist countries of Europe, a place is found for what is variously called 'manual work' or 'work-experience'. In our country, a revolutionary experiment was launched by Mahatma Gandhi in the form of basic education. The concept of work-experience is essentially similar. It may be described as a redefinition of his educational thinking in terms of a society on the road to industrialization. In addition to being an effective educational tool, workexperience can, serve some other important purposes.

It can help to make the distinction between intellectual and manual work less marked as also the social stratification based on it. It could make the entry of youth into the world of work and employment easier by enabling them to adjust themselves to it. It could contribute to the increase of national productivity both by helping students to develop insights into productive processes and the use of science, and by generating in them the habit of hard and responsible work. And it might help social and national integration by strengthening the links between the individual and the community and by creating bonds of understanding between the educated persons and the masses.

In providing work-experience, every attempt should be made to link programmes realistically to technology, to industrialization and to the application of science to productive processes, including agriculture. This 'forward look' in work-experience is important for a country which has embarked on a programme of industrialization. These problems will be discussed in detail elsewhere.

In a well-organized programme, work-experience, at least from the higher primary stage, should also result in some earning for the student-either in cash or in kind. This would meet, to Some extent, the expenditure which the students have to incur on their education or on their maintenance while at study. The amount of this earning will naturally increase as the students go up the educational ladder and it becomes possible to organize work-experience in a manner that would enable them to 'earn and learn'.

The ultimate objective should be to move towards a situation in which the education. of a student is not held to be complete unless he participates in some type of work-experience in real-life conditions and earns some amount, however small, towards his own maintenance. This will also help to develop in him values which promote economic growth, such as appreciating the importance of productive work and manual labour, willingness and capacity for hard work, and thrift.

Vocationalization

Another programme which can bring education into closer relationship with productivity is to give a strong vocational bias to secondary education and to increase the emphasis on agricultural and technological education at the university stage. This is of special significance in the Indian situation. where, as the Kothari Commision have pointed out, the educational system has been training young persons so far mostly for government services and the so-called whitecollar professions. The introduction of practical subjects in secondary schools so as to divert them into different walks of life was first recommended, as far back as in 1882, by the Indian Education Commission. But little or no effective action was taken to implement the recommendations and even today the enrolment in the vocational courses at the secondary stage is only nine per cent of the total enrolment, which is among the lowest in the world. Even at the university stage, vocational education (other than for law, medicine, or teaching) was mostly ignored throughout the last century.

Even as late as in 1917, the Calcutta University Commission pointed out that the great majority of university students about 22,000 out of 26,000pursue purely literary courses which do not fit them for any but administrative, clerical, teaching and (indirectly) legal careers.

About fifty years later, we find that the overall picture has improved only slightly and the proportion of students at the university stage enrolled in all courses of professional education is only 23 per cent of the total enrolment. The Kothari Commision's proposals on this subject are discussed elsewhere. But it may be briefly stated here that the Commision visualize the future trend of school education to be towards a fruitful mingling of general and vocational education-general education containing some elements of pre-vocational and technical education, and vocational education, in its turn, having an element of general education. In the kind of society in which we will be living in the coming years, a complete separation between the two will not only be undesirable but impossible. The Commision also expected a considerable expansion of professional education at the university stage, especially in the agricultural and technological fields.

Education and Social and National Integration

Social and national integration is crucial to the creation of a strong, united country, which is an essential pre-condition for all progress. It has a varied content-economic, social, cultural and political-and its different facets are closely interconnected. It needs:

— confidence in the nation's future;

— a continuous rise in the standard of living for the masses and the reduction in unemployment and in the disparities in development between different parts of the country, all of which are essential to promote a sense of equality of opportunity in political, economic and social terms;

— a deep sense of the values and obligations of citizenship and a growing identification of the people, not with sectional loyalties but with the 'nation' as a whole;

— assurance of good and impartial administration, equal treatment for every citizen, in fact and not merely in law, based on the integrity of the public services; and

— mutual understanding of and respect for the culture, traditions and ways of life of different sections of the nation.

To make this social and psychological revolution possible, it is necessary to deal with the short-term problems facing the country in this field, particularly in regard to the growing and dangerous symptoms of social disorganization. These express themselves as the widening gulf between the rich and the poor, the privileged and the unprivileged, the urban and the rural, the educated and the uneducated. They are reflected in the general weakening of the feeling of national solidarity under the increasing impact of local, regional, linguistic, religious and other sectional or parochial loyalties. Effective steps must be taken to bridge these dangerous gulfs and strengthen national consciousness and unity.

Social and national integration is a major problem which will have to be tackled on several fronts, including education. In the Kothari Commision's view, education can and should play a very significant role in it by

— introducing a common school system of public education;
— making social and national service an integral part of education at all stages;
— developing all modem Indian languages, and taking necessary steps to enrich Hindi as quickly as possible so that it is able to function effectively as the official language of the Union; and
— promoting national consciousness.

The Common School

In a situation of the type we have ill India, it is the responsibility of the educational system to bring the different social classes and groups together and thus promote the emergence of an egalitarian and integrated society. But at present instead of doing so, education itself is tending to increase social segregation and to perpetuate and widen class distinctions. At the primary stage, the free schools to which the masses send their children are maintained by the government and local authorities and are generally of poor quality. Some of the private schools are definitely better; but since many of them charge high fees, they are availed of only by the middle and the higher classes. At the secondary stage, a large proportion of the good schools are private but many of them also charge high fees which are normally beyond the means of any but the top ten per cent of the people, though some of the middle class parents make great sacrifices to send their children to them. There is thus segregation in education itself-the minority of private, fee-charging, better schools meeting the needs of the upper classes and the vast bulk of free, publicly maintained, but poor schools being utilized by the rest. What is worse, this segregation is 'increasing and tending to widen the gulf between the classes and the masses.

This is one of the major weaknesses of the existing educational system. Good education, instead of being available to all children, or at least to all the able children from every stratum of society, is available only to a small minority which is usually selected not on the basis of talent but on the basis of its capacity to pay fees. The identification and development of the total national pool of ability is greatly hampered. The position is thus undemocratic and inconsistent with the ideal of an egalitarian society. The children of the masses are compelled to receive substandard education and, as the programme of scholarships is not very large sometimes even the ablest among them are unable to find access to such good schools as exist, while the economically privileged parents are able to 'buy' good education for their children. This is bad not only for the children of the poor but also for the children from the rich and privileged groups. It gives them a short-term advantage in so far as it enables them to perpetuate and consolidate their position. But it must be realized that, in the long run, their self-interest lies in identifying themselves with the masses. By segregating their children, such privileged parents prevent them from sharing the life and experiences of the children of the poor and coming into contact with the realities of life. In addition to weakening social cohesion, they also render the education of their own children anaemic and incomplete.

If these evils are to be eliminated and the educational system is to become a powerful instrument of national development in general, and social and national integration in particular, we must move towards the goal of a common school system of public education which will be open to all children, irrespective of caste, creed, community, religion, economic conditions or social status;

— where access to good education will depend not oil wealth or class but on talent;
— which will maintain adequate standards in all schools and provide at least a reasonable proportion of quality institutions;
— in which no tuition fee will be charged; and
— which would meet the needs of the average parent so that he would not ordinarily feel the need to send his children to expensive schools outside the system.

Such an educational system has, for instance, been built up in the USSR and is one of the major factors which have contributed to its progress. It has also been developed, in different forms and to varying degrees, in other nations like the USA, France and the Scandinavian countries. The traditional English system has been different and has allowed good education, under private management, to be largely reserved for those who have the capacity to pay the necessary fees. But recently, the so-called Public Schools have come in for strong criticism in England itself and it is not unlikely that a radical change may be initiated to make them more democratic. A somewhat similar system was transplanted in India by British administrators and we have clung to it so long because it happened to be in tune with the traditional hierarchical structure of our society. Whatever its past history may be, such a system has no valid place in the new democratic and socialistic society we desire to create.

Social and National Service

The present educational system is also responsible for

increasing the gulf between the educated and the uneducated classes, between the intelligentsia and the masses. The intelligentsia should try to become a real service-group striving to uplift the masses and should resist the temptation to become a parasitical group living for itself and perpetuating its own privileged position. Our traditional 'elite' as a whole-with some noble exceptions-had no close ties with the masses, and the new 'elite' created by modern education also remained largely aloof from the people, except during the struggle for freedom under Mahatma Gandhi when he was able to inspire large numbers of educated and even well-to-do persons to identify themselves with the interests of the masses and the country as a whole. But from the time the struggle for freedom came to an end with the attainment of independence, they have again tended to move away from the people. This is a great danger and, with a view to meeting it, suitable programmes to help in the evolution of a well-knit and united nation have to be devised.

Programmes of social and national service can be organized in one of two ways: they can either be carried out occasionally on a part-time basis during the period of education, or organized as a period of full-time service in addition to the present period of education. The second approach was recommended by the National Service Committee appointed under the chairmanship of Dr. C. D. Deshmukh. It was suggested that national service should be a fulltime programme of nine to twelve months for all young persons (except for those allowed deferment on valid academic or other grounds) after passing out of higher secondary schools or the pre-university course and before entering employment or the university. The programme was to include some military training, social service, manual labour and general education. These proposals have not been adopted so far; nor have the public reactions to them been very favourable. Instead, at the time of the national emergency (1962), the scheme of compulsory National Cadet Corps (NCC) was introduced at the university stage.

Instead of adding one year to the total span of education for the purpose, a more feasible plan may be to develop, as an integral part of education, a programme which would run concurrently with academic studies in school and college. The programme should begin from the upper primary stage and continue up to the university so that the emphasized in the socialistic pattern of society, which the nation desires to create, is that individual fulfilment will come, not through selfish and narrow loyalties to personal or group interests, but through the dedication of all to the wider loyalties of national development in all its parameters.

There are two main forms in which such service can be organized:

— encouraging and enabling students to participate in community living on the school or college campus; and

— providing opportunities of participation in programmes of community development and national service.

Community Living in Schools and Colleges

Every educational institution should try to develop a rich community life of its own and provide adequate and satisfying opportunities for students to participate in it and help in organizing it. Various opportunities for such work exist in the classroom, on the campuses of the schools and the colleges. in the hostels and on the playgrounds. For instance, instead of utilizing servants and hired labour for educational institutions and their hostels, it is possible to have much of the work done by students, not primarily to save money, but to provide valuable experience. Japan has followed this Practice in her national system, and many schools in India (including some schools for well-to-do children) are also doing so to some extent. This type of work-experience would cultivate in students the habit of work and a sense of the dignity of labour. If this is done on a nation-wide scale, it will incidentally effect some saving in expenditure which could be utilized for providing certain basic amenities for students. The training institutions for basic teachers have tried to develop such traditions of community living by eliminating the use of servants to a large extent. The Kothari Commision recommend that this pattern of hostel life should be introduced in all schools and colleges so far as possible. The practice of making self-help and manual work a part of the daily life and training in all types of educational institutions-as was the case in many of the old Ashrams and Academies-would yield good educational results.

Participation in Programmes of Community Development

In addition to these institutional programmes, it is essential to make participation in meaningful programmes of community service an integral part of all education from the primary to the undergraduate stage. Such participation can help to create positive attitudes towards social service and to develop closer ties between the educated persons and the rest of the people. It can also help in building up a sense of social purpose and self-confidence and giving students a sense of participation in community life and activities.

The organization of the programmes will naturally vary from stage to stage:

(1) At the primary stage, it will take the form of bringing the school closer to the community with an accent on serving the community in suitable ways.

(2) At the secondary stage, such programmes can be more ambitiously designed, and have a greater impact on young minds. Every secondary school should develop carefully planned programmes for promoting good school-community relations and suitable forms of service to the community. The Kothari Commision recommend that about ten days a year (or a total of 30 days at the lower secondary stage and 20 days at the higher secondary stage) may be fully devoted to such programmes. Where this is not possible, it should be obligatory for the students to participate in the Labour Service Camps for secondary school students to be organized by the State Education Departments on a district basis. The programme is discussed more fully elsewhere.

(3) Similarly, it should be obligatory for every college student, before he is awarded his first degree, to put in at least 60 days of national service in one to three stretches. Each college should develop its own programme, suited to its objectives, its resources and the age and competence of its students. Participation in Labour and Social Welfare Camps or the NCC should also be regarded as alternative forms of such service.

The NCC programme, which has been made compulsory at the university stage during the last three years, has shown some good results. It has possibilities of promoting national development by building up closer ties between the people and the defence services. It also helps to lessen the difference between the so-called 'martial' and other classes and inculcates the idea of the defence of freedom in all classes of people.

Evolution of a Language Policy

The development of a proper language policy can also

assist materially in social and national integration. Of the many problems which the country has faced since independence, the language question has been one of the most complex and intractable, and it still continues to be so. Its early and satisfactory solution is imperative for a variety of reasonseducational, cultural and political.

It is hardly necessary to emphasize that the development of the Indian languages is both urgent and essential for the development of the Indian people and as a way of bringing together the elite and the masses. It can make scientific and technical knowledge more easily accessible to the people in their own languages and thus help not only in the progress of industrialization but also in the wider dissemination of science and the scientific outlook. Energetic action is needed to produce books and literature, particularly scientific and technical, in the regional languages. This should be regarded as a specific and imperative responsibility of the universities; and the UGC should provide general guidance and allot adequate funds for the programme.

Medium of Education in Schools and Colleges

The development of the modem Indian languages is inextricably linked with the importance given to them in the educational system, specially at the university stage. The medium selected should enable students to acquire knowledge with facility, to express themselves with clarity and to think with precision and vigour. From this point of view, the claims of the mother-tongue are preeminent. About thirty years ago, delivering the convocation address of the Calcutta University, Rabindra Nath Tagore had expressed Ms views in this matter in no uncertain terms:

In no country in the world, except India, is to be seen this divorce of the language of education from the language of the pupil. Full hundred years have not elapsed since Japan took its initiation into Western culture. At the outset she had to take recourse to textbooks written in foreign languages, but from the very first, her objective had been to arrive at the stage of ranging freely over the subjects of study in the language of the country. It was because Japan had recognized the need of such studies, not as an ornament for a select section of her citizens, but for giving power and culture to all of them, that she deemed it to be of prime importance to make them universally available to her people. And in this effort of Japan to gain proficiency in the Western arts and sciences, which was to give her the means of self-defence against the predatory cupidity of foreign powers, to qualify her to take an honoured place in the comity of nations, no trouble or expense was spared. Least of all was there the miserly folly of keeping such learning out of easy reach, within the confines of a foreign language.

Learning through a foreign medium compels the students to concentrate on cramming instead of mastering the subject-matter. Moreover, as a matter of sound educational policy, the medium of education in school and higher education should generally be the same. Prior to 1937, the position was at least consistent. English was the medium both in the upper stages of school and college education.

It has been sometimes argued that there should be a single medium of education at the university stage-English for the time being, to be ultimately replaced by Hindi-on the ground that it would promote mobility of teachers and students from one part of the country to another, provide for easy communication between academic and professional men and administrators, further intellectual cooperation amongst the universities and help in other ways in developing a corporate intellectual life in the country. This solution is not feasible. In practice, it will probably mean the indefinite continuance of English as the only medium of higher education, a development that we cannot support in the larger interests of the country. The adoption of Hindi as a common medium of education in all parts of India is not possible for some years to come, and in non-Hindi areas it will still have some of the disadvantages associated with the use of a foreign medium and is likely to be resisted. It would, therefore, be unwise to strive to reverse the present trend for the adoption of the regional languages as media of education at the university stage and to insist on the use of a common medium in higher education throughout the country.

EDUCATION AND MODERNIZATION

The most distinctive feature of a modern society, in contrast with a traditional one, is in its adoption of a science-based technology. It is this which has helped such societies to increase their production so spectacularly. It may be pointed out, however, that science-based technology has other important implications for social and cultural life and it involves fundamental social and cultural changes which are broadly described as 'modernization'.

Explosion of Knowledge

There has been a great explosion of knowledge during the last few decades. In a traditional society, the stock of knowledge is limited and grows slowly so that the main aim of education is interpreted to be its preservation. In a modern society, on the other hand, the stock of knowledge is far greater and the pace of its growth is infinitely quicker. One of the main tasks of education ill a modern society is to keep pace with this advance in knowledge. In such a society, knowledge inevitably ceases to be something to be received passively; it is something to be actively discovered. If this is rightly understood, it would involve a revolution in traditional education where 'to know' has come to mean 'to know by heart', where respect for all inherited knowledge is assiduously cultivated and where the assimilative faculties tend to be emphasized to the neglect of the critical and creative ones. In India, as in other countries where similar conditions prevail, this would require, among other things, a new approach to the objectives and methods of education, and changes in the training of teachers. Unless they are trained in new ways of teaching and learning, the students in schools and colleges will not be able to receive the type of education needed for the new society.

Rapid Social Change

Another feature of a modern society is the quick, almost breath-taking rate at which social change takes place. In a traditional society, change is so slow that the conservatism of the educational system does comparatively little harm. ID a modern society, on the other hand, change is so rapid that the school must always be alert if it is to keep abreast of significant changes. There is, therefore, an imperative need for adopting a dynamic policy in such a situation. An educational system which does not continually renovate itself, becomes out of date and hampers progress because it tends to create a lag between its operative purposes and standards and the new imperatives of development, both in quality and quantity. The very aim of education has to be viewed differently-it is no longer taken as concerned primarily with the imparting of knowledge or the preparation of a finished product, but with the awakening of curiosity, the development of proper interests, attitudes and values and the building up of such essential skills as independent study and the capacity to think and judge for oneself without which it is not possible to become a responsible member of a democratic society.

Need for Rapid Advance

Two other aspects of modernization need emphasis. The first is that once a society launches itself upon a programme of modernization, there is no turning back, no half-way house where we can arrest the process. In the initial stages, such a change must disturb the traditional equilibrium reached and maintained over centuries which, though it had its obvious disadvantages, had some built-in redeeming factors as well. The attempt to create a new social order naturally creates a host of unexpected social, economic, cultural and political problems. But if one tinkers with the problems involved or tries to march with faltering steps, if one's commitments and convictions are half-hearted and faith is lacking, the new situation may turn out to be worse than the old one. The only solution to these transitional problems is to move rapidly forward and create a new equilibrium, based on the full implications of the process of modernization.

Modernization and Educational Progress

The progress of modernization will, therefore, be directly related to the pace of educational advance and the one sure way to modernize quickly is to spread education, produce educated and skilled citizens, and train an adequate and competent intelligentsia. The Indian society of today is heir to a great culture. Unfortunately, however, it is not an adequately educated society, and unless it becomes one, it will not be able to modernize itself and to respond appropriately to the new challenges of national reconstruction or take its rightful place in the comity of nations. The proportion of persons who have so far been able to receive secondary and higher education is very small at present-less than two per cent of the entire population. This will have to be increased to at least ten per cent to make any significant impact. The composition of the intelligentsia must also be changed; it should consist of able persons, both men and women, drawn from all strata of society. There must also be changes in the skills and fields of specialization to be cultivated. At present, the intelligentsia consists predominantly of the white-collar professions and students of the humanities, while the proportion of scientists and technical workers in its ranks is quite small. To change this, greater emphasis must be placed, on vocational subjects, science education and research. The average level of competence is not at all satisfactory, due mainly to inadequate standards maintained in the universities. This is damaging to Indian academic life and its reputation. In order to change this situation radically, it will be necessary to establish a few 'major' universities in the country which attain standards comparable to the best in any part of the world, and which will gradually spread their influence to others. This is one of the basic reforms needed in our system of higher education.

Morals and Values in Education

Modernization does not mean-least of all in our national situation-a refusal to recognize the importance of or to inculcate necessary moral and spiritual values and self-discipline. Modernization, if it is to be a living force, must derive its strength from the strength of the spirit. Modernization aims, amongst other things, at creating an economy of plenty which will offer to every individual a larger way of life and a wider variety of choices.While this freedom to choose has its own advantages, it also means that the future of society will depend increasingly upon the type of choice each individual makes. This would naturally depend upon his motivation and sense of values, for he might make the choice either with reference entirely to his own personal satisfaction or in a spirit of service to the community and of furthering the common good.

The expanding knowledge and the growing power which modernization places at the disposal of society must, therefore, be combined with the strengthening and deepening of the sense of social responsibility and a keener appreciation of moral and spiritual values. While a combination of ignorance with goodness may be futile, that of knowledge with a lack of essential values may be dangerous. The weakening of social and moral values in the younger generation is creating many serious social and ethical conflicts in western societies and there is already a desire among some great western thinkers to balance the knowledge and skills which science and technology bring with the values and insights associated with ethics and religion at Its best, viz., a search for the knowledge of the Self, of the meaning of life, of the relationship of man to other human beings and to the ultimate reality. in the situation that is developing it is equally important for us to give a proper valueorientation to our educational system.

The University Education Commission (1948) considered both its philosophical and practical aspects and made certain valuable proposals for reform. However, except in a small Dumber of 'institutions, they were not implemented. In 1959 the Central Advisory Board of Education appointed a special committee on Religious and Moral Instruction.In the attempt to inculcate values through education, we should draw freely upon our own traditions as well as the traditions of other countries and cultures. There are strands within Indian thought itself which can lead to the new outlook appropriate for a modern society and which can prepare the people for a willing acceptance of life with all its joys and sorrows, its challenges and triumphs. In them, too, we can find inspiration for social service and a faith in the future.

Mahatma Gandhi, for instance-and some other great leaders of thought-discovered the inspiration for their idealism and their passionate striving for social justice and social reconstruction largely from these sources. It is such reinterpretations and re-evaluations of the past that are now most needed. It is, however, specially important in the world of today that this effort should not be restricted to the national sources only. It would be necessary to draw upon the liberalizing forces that have arisen in the western nations and which have emphasized, among other things, the dignity of the individual, equality and social justice, e.g., the French Revolution, the concept of the welfare state, the philosophy of Marx and the rise of socialism.

A major weakness of the Indian, and particularly of the Hindu society, in the past has been a lack of equality and social justice. These balancing influences have, therefore, a great significance. Similar assimilations of whatever is significant should also be discriminatingly made from other important nations and cultures such as the Chinese, Japanese or Islamic.

Secularism and Religion

In a multi-religious society like ours, it is necessary to define the attitude of the State to religion, religious education and the concept of secularism. The adoption of a secularist policy means that in political, economic and social matters, all citizens, irrespective of their religious faith, will enjoy equality of rights, that no religious community will be favoured or discriminated against, and that instruction in religious dogmas will not be provided in State schools. But it is not an irreligious or anti-religious policy; it does not belittle the importance of religion as such. it gives to every citizen the fullest freedom of religious belief and worship. It is anxious to ensure good relations amongst different religious groups and to promote not only religious tolerance but also an active reverence for all religions.

In such a society, however, one has to make a distinction between religious education' and 'education about religions'. The former is largely concerned with the teaching of the tenets and practices of a particular religion, generally in the form in which the religious group envisages them, whereas the latter is a study of religions and religious thought from a broad point of view-the eternal quest of the spirit. it would not be practicable for a secular State with many religions to provide education in any one religion. It is, however, necessary for a multi-religious democratic State to promote a tolerant study of all religions so that its citizens can understand each other better and live amicably together. It must be remembered that, owing to the ban placed on religious instruction in schools and the weakening of the home influences which, in the past, often provided such instruction, children are now growing up without any clear idea of their Own religion and with no chance of learning about others. In fact, the general ignorance and misunderstanding in these matters are so widespread in the younger generation as to 'De fraught with great danger for the development of a democracy in which tolerance is rated high as a value. The Kothari Commision suggest that a syllabus giving well-chosen information about each of the major religions should be included as a part of the course in citizenship or as part of the general. education to be introduced in schools and colleges up to the first degree.

It should highlight the fundamental similarities in the great religions of the world and the emphasis they place on the cultivation of certain broadly comparable moral and spiritual values. It would be a great advantage to have a common course on this subject in all parts of the country and common textbooks which should be prepared at the national level by competent and suitable experts on each religion. When these courses have been prepared, it would be worth while to have them scrutinized by a small committee of eminent persons belonging to different religions to ensure that nothing is included in them to which any religious group could take legitimate objection.

A vitalized study of science with its emphasis on openmindedness, tolerance and objectivity would inevitably lead to the development of a more secular outlook, in the sense in which we use the word, amongst those who profess different religions. This process needs to be carefully and wisely encouraged. Simultaneously, there is a sense in which the walls between the secular and the spiritual are tending to break down and what is secular is seen to have spiritual roots. In the words of Dr. Iqbal, 'the spirit finds its opportunity in the material, the natural and the secular. All that is secular is, therefore, sacred in the roots of its being'. This is what the Kothari Commision envisage as the direction of our future development. The Commision believed that India should strive to bring science and the values of the spirit together and in harmony, and thereby pave the way for the eventual emergence of a society which would cater to the needs of the whole man and not only to a particular fragment of his personality.

India is on the move again-with the promise of a new renaissance in the making. After a long period of foreign rule she has emerged into freedom. That her means for the winning of freedom, adopted under

Gandhi and Nehru, were as noble as the ends, is a signpost of profound historical significance.

Politically the land is free, but economically she has a long, way to go. The elimination of ignorance and of grinding poverty accumulated over centuries of inertia and exploitation is not an easy task. India today has half of the total illiterate population of the world.. About fifty million of her people, a tenth of the total population, live on an yearly income of no more than Rs. 120. The problems are grave and immense. But this is only one side of the picture. During recent, years, great strides have been taken towards industrialization, towards modernization of agriculture, and to provide better health and life to the people.

The· most powerful tool in the process of modernization is education based on science and technology. The one great lesson of the present age of science is that, with determination and the willingness to put in hard work, prosperity' within the reach of any nation which has a stable and progressive government. There is no doubt that in the years to come India's trade and commerce will grow: there will be more food for all, more education, better health; and a reasonable standard of living will be available. But India's contribution can and should be far more than these material gains. She should learn to harness science but she must also learn not to be dominated by science.

In this respect India has a unique advantage with her great tradition of duty without self-involvement unacquisitive temperament tolerance, and innate love of peace and reverence for all living things. Too often are these precious assets forgotten and we tend to relapse into moods of pessimism, fears and forebodings, discord and destructive criticism. A new pride and a deeper faith expressed in living for the noble ideals of peace and freedom, truth and compassion, are now needed.

4

Standards of Educational System

The standards in any given system of education at a given time depend upon four elements:

(1) the structure or the division of the educational pyramid into different levels or stages and their interrelationships;

(2) the duration or total period covered by the different stages;

(3) the extent and quality of essential inputs such as teachers, curricula, methods of teaching and evaluation, equipment and buildings; and

(4) the utilization of available facilities.

All these elements are interrelated, but they are not of equal significance. For instance, the structure, which may be regarded as the skeleton of the educational system, is of the least importance. The duration or total period of education plays a more significant role; but it becomes crucial only when the available facilities are utilized to the full and no further improvement can be expected without the addition of time. The quality of different inputs is even more important, and with an improvement in these, it is possible to raise the standards considerably without affecting the structure or increasing the duration. But the utilization of available facilities is probably the most significant of all the elements on which standards depend. For any self-accelerating process of development, it is essential in the first place to improve efficiency at the level of the existing inputs and to add more inputs only if they are crucial to the process. An increase of inputs assumes significance only at a later stage.

In this context, it may be interesting to note that until recently, the general tendency everywhere has been to overrate the importance of the duration of the school course. There is a reason for this. When the quantum of knowledge covered in the school was not very large, the pace of school work was leisurely, and when one learnt more outside school than within school, it was natural to suppose that the longer one stayed at school the better one gained in knowledge and maturity. All this has changed now. The knowledge explosion has imposed an altogether new pressure on schools and colleges. Formal education now plays a much greater part than it did previously at any time in history and the efficiency of the educational system has become a very important factor.

Machlup, in his monumental study on the Production and Distribution of Knowledge in the United States has observed that the learning process in school in the United States could and ought to be accelerated. He has vigorously argued that the educational objectives now attained in 12 years of schooling could be achieved in 9 or 10 years. This would mean a saving every year of tens of billions of dollars. Besides, it will save the precious time of students and teachers. This 'timesaving' is becoming increasingly important as there is so much more to learn in a fast knowledge-expanding world. The compression of the school course would also help in the development of satisfactory working habits and powers of concentration and application.

Many people are impressed by the fact that the Soviet Union's ten-year cycle of primary and secondary education requires that all students must take five years of physics, six years of mathematics, three years of biology, and four years of chemistry, with the course content of the work during the last two years being comparable to that of the usual introductory courses in these subjects offered in our liberal arts colleges. By contrast our corresponding school period contains twelve rather than ten years but provides on the average only one-fifth as much training in mathematics and the sciences. There is insufficient evidence to show that the intensity of early Soviet scientific training is either necessary or desirable, particularly if it involves sacrifices of some emphasis on the humanities, but it is evident that the standard programme in our schools is far from optimum.

The questions on structure and duration were those on which the Commission received perhaps the largest volume of advice and suggestions. They are questions to which previous commissions and committees dealing with the problems of education on a national scale have devoted considerable attention. There are two principal reasons for this widespread and continuous concern about the structure of the educational system. One is the general desire that the present somewhat confusing variety of patterns of school and higher education should be ended. The other is the popular belief that the total period of the educational course and the duration of its different stages have a direct bearing on the quality of the education imparted. If there is a uniformity in the educational pattern and an extension in the total period of schooling, it will be possible to bring about a general rise in the standards of attainment. These contentions are of considerable importance and merit close examination.

Higher Secondary Pattern

It may be instructive in this connection to look briefly at the results of one serious effort made since Independence to carry out a plan for the reorganization of the educational structure. As a result of the Report of the Secondary Education Commission, a decision was taken to develop a national pattern of school classes covering eleven years-five years of lower primary, three years of upper primary and three years of higher secondary classes. This was to be followed by a three-year course for the first degree in arts and science and a further two-year course for the second degree.

The upgrading of high schools in accordance with what is popularly known as the higher secondary pattern and the introduction of the three-year degree course in universities have been significant changes in the educational structure over the last ten years. But while the three-year degree course has been introduced everywhere except in the State of Uttar Pradesh 15 and the University of Bombay, the same success has not attended the efforts to convert high schools into higher secondary schools.

In spite of the offer of Central assistance, only five States have implemented the proposal so far, while the others have either not accepted it at all, or having decided to accept it in the first instance, have gone back on their earlier decision. Only about 25 per cent of the total number of secondary schools in the country were converted to the higher secondary pattern by the end of the third plan. Many of these conversions are purely notional in the sense that the necessary facilities in terms of teachers, libraries and laboratories have not yet been provided. What is particularly relevant to our discussion here is that no uniform pattern of school and college classes has emerged as a result of the reorganization and there is almost as great a variety of patterns today as there was when the scheme of reorganization was first launched.

Uniformity of Pattern

A number of different proposals for the reorganization of the educational structure were placed before the Commission. Most of these recommended a uniform pattern of school and college classes in all parts of the country. It may be pointed out in this connection that the Committee on Emotional Integration stated in their Report as follows:

The Commission have recommended certain steps that should be taken for the coordination of educational standards at the school stage in the different States. There are several characteristic features of the Indian situation, such as the vastness of the country and the immense diversity of local conditions and traditions, that demand a certain element of flexibility in the educational structure. Even in a country of small size such as the United Kingdom, for example, the pattern in England (generally thirteen years of school education followed by a three-year course for the first degree) is different from that in Scotland (twelve years of school education followed by a four-year course for the first degree). In our country, where the different States are at unequal levels of development, a uniform pattern might be above the resources and real needs of the backward areas and below the capacity and requirements of the advanced areas and might operate to the disadvantage of both.

A second popular demand that has been stressed in proposals for structural reorganization received by the Commission, is related to lengthening the total duration of school and higher education. This demand, it may be pointed out, is not related to the professional degrees such as engineering or medicine, the total duration of the study for which is not less than 16 years and is about the same as in most of the educationally advanced countries. This demand 'only refers to the first degrees in arts and science, which are now taken four years after the matriculation or an equivalent examination, and the contention put forward is that this duration should be lengthened to not less than five years after the matriculation. This view, it must be pointed Out, accords with the thinking of several expert bodies on the subject.

As far back as in 1919, the Calcutta University Commission proposed that the dividing line between the university and the secondary school should be drawn at the intermediate examination, which came after twelve years of education. Similarly, the University Education Commission recommended that students should be admitted to the university after the completion of twelve years of study, and that the first degree course should be of three years' duration.

According to the Committee on Emotional Integration, the eleven-year period of school education was inadequate preparation for entrance to the university, and the lengthening of the course by one year was deemed necessary. At the conference of the State Education Ministers held in 1964, it was resolved that 'a twelve-year course of schooling before admission to the degree course was the goal towards which the country must work'.

Reorganization of the Educational Structure

The kind of reorganization suggested above, which involves a lengthening of the duration of school education, cannot obviously be effected within a short period. The vastness of the country and the variety of its educational patterns make the task a formidable one, and the pressure of more urgent claims on the limited educational resources adds to the complexity of the problem.

The Kothari commision recommended that the reorganization should be carried out through a phased programme spread over at least twenty years. The first step in this direction would be the abandoning of the present higher secondary pattern in which specialization begins in class IX, and the institution of a new higher secondary course beginning in class Xi. Along with this measure, which should be completed by the end of the Fourth Plan period, a systematic attempt should be made to transfer the pre-university course at present located in universities and affiliated colleges, where it tends to depress standards of higher education, to secondary schools, where it rightly belongs. The next step would be to lengthen the total duration by adding a year to the higher secondary course.

The Commission visualize a flexible educational structure covering

- a pre-school stage of one to three years;
- a primary stage of seven or eight years divided into two sub-stages-a lower primary stage of four or five years and a higher Primary stage of three years
- a lower secondary or high school stage of three or two years in general education or of one to three years in vocational education;
- a higher secondary stage of two years of general education or one to three years of vocational education;
- a higher education stage having a course of three years or more for the first degree, followed by courses of varying durations for the second or research degrees.

The First Ten Years

The primary and secondary schools will be of various

types. The largest single group amongst them will consist of lower primary schools. A smaller number-about one in three-will provide education up to the end of the higher primary stage and these would necessarily include the lower classes. When the present higher secondary pattern is abandoned, most of the secondary schools-about three-fourths-would provide education up to class X and may begin at any convenient point lower down; and the remaining onefourth will be higher secondary schools providing education up to university entrance.

The existing position, however, is quite different from this and shows considerable variations in the structure of the school system until the public examination at the end of the lower secondary stage is reached. A reference to chart on page 55 shows that this external examination, which is known by different names but which we shall call the high school examination, comes after ten to twelve years: two States (Assam and Nagaland) have the examination after twelve years; six States (Andhra Pradesh, Bihar, Gujarat, Madras, Maharashtra and Orissa) have it after eleven years; and the remaining eight States (Jammu & Kashmir, Kerala, Madhya Pradesh,17 Mysore, Punjab, Rajasthan, Uttar Pradesh and West Bengal) have it after ten years. No systematic study has yet been made for comparing the standards of attainment of the candidates at the examinations held in the different regions. But these are broadly comparable and, for administrative purposes, all these examinations are regarded as equivalent.

It will be seen from the chart that in Assam and Nagaland, the first two classes are called A and B, and it is the next ten classes that are numbered consecutively as classes I to X. Since the Governments of the two States themselves seem to treat classes A and B as Infant classes and separate them from the other ten classes, the school stage leading to the high school examination in these

States may be regarded as covering a period of ten years. In the six States which have an eleven-year school course, it is more appropriate to regard class I as a pre-primary class, particularly where the age of admission is less than six years.

According to the Kothari commission, the pre-primary class is an advantage which these States possess. The commission recommended that they should try to retain it as such, organize the learning experiences therein on the play-way pattern rather than on the formal pattern, and extend it downwards, wherever possible, to cover a period of two years. The commission also suggest that the other eight States may try to provide pre-primary education of one year or more below class I to the extent possible, subject to the availability of financial resources.

(1) the first ten years of schooling, covering a primary stage of seven or eight years and a lower secondary stage of three or two years, will provide a course of general education without any specialization;

(2) the primary stage will be Preceded, wherever possible, by pre-primary education of one to three years;

(3) the age of admission to class I will ordinarily be not less than 6+;

(4) at the end of the primary stage, a proportion of students will step off the school system and enter working life (about 20 per cent); some more will step out off the stream of general education into different vocational courses whose duration may range from one to three years (about 20 per cent); and those remaining will continue further in the stream of general education (about 60 per cent);

(5) the ten years of school education will be followed by all external examination;

(6) the standard at the end of the ten years will be broadly comparable in respect of curriculum and level of attainment to the national standard laid down for the end of this stage;

(7) at the end of the ten years of school education, a proportion of students will step off the school system and enter working life (about 40 per cent); some more will step out off the stream of general education and enter vocational courses =duration will be one to three years (about 30 per cent); and those remaining will continue further in the stream of general education whose duration will be one, and ultimately two years (about 30 per cent).

Modification of Higher Secondary System

The Commission attach great significance to changes that have to be made in the existing higher secondary pattern in the light of the proposals for reorganization made above.

(1) The system of 'streaming' in schools of general education, which now begins in class IX, should be given up and no attempt at specialization should be made till after class X. This will need a considerable reorganization of the existing curricula of the higher secondary schools.

(2) The idea that every secondary school should be raised to the higher secondary status should also be abandoned. It has been possible to upgrade all the high schools in Delhi because it is a metropolitan area. Such wholesale conversion of schools has also been carried out in Madhya Pradesh; but the cost has been very heavy in terms of deterioration of standards as well as of financial outlays. In a country where rural areas predominate, it is unwise to try to raise every high school to the higher secondary

status. With a view to concentrating resources and raising standards effectively, it is only the bigger and better type of high school that should be upgraded. If one-fourth of the total number of high schools were raised to the higher secondary status, they would meet all the needs of the situation, even on the assumption that there would be no pre-university courses in the colleges in the future. An essential requirement is that the institutions should be large, centrally located and equitably distributed between the urban and the rural areas. It would also be desirable to review the status of all existing higher secondary schools, and where these are too small and uneconomic or of very poor quality, they may be reconverted into high schools.

(3) There should be, as a rule, no integrated course of studies beginning with class IX. Classes IX and X will now form part of the first ten years of general education, and classes XI and XII (and during the transitional period, class XI only), which will provide for specialized studies in different subjects at the higher secondary stage, will become an independent, self-contained unit like the Sixth Form in England.

(4) There will be an external examination at the end of class X to mark the termination of the first ten years of general education. Therefore, a student studying in a ten-year high school will have to appear for two external examinations at the end of classes X and XI-at the interval of one year. This handicap will be removed with the extension of the higher secondary course to two years.

(5) Existing higher secondary schools with a well-organized integrated course in classes IX to XI may be permitted to carry on, if they so desire, with such a course until they add class XII. It will not be

obligatory for the students of such schools to appear for an examination at the end of class X. They may take one final examination at the end of class XI or take it in two parts at the end of classes X and XI.

Vocational Courses

It has been stated above that about 20 per cent of the students will leave the educational system and join working life at the end of the primary stage and that about an equal proportion will step off from the stream of general education and join vocational courses. It will be necessary to provide adequate facilities for suitable forms of vocational education, either on a part-time or on a full-time basis, for these students. This problem will be discussed in greater detail elsewhere.

Courses Corresponding to Higher Secondary Stage

The name, duration, location and control of courses corresponding to the higher secondary stage vary from State to State. In Uttar Pradesh, the course is designated as 'Intermediate' and the duration is two years. It is located either in the top classes of secondary schools or in the bottom classes of degree colleges. and its academic control is vested in the Board of High School and Intermediate Examinations.

In Kerala,, the course is provided in institutions called 'Junior Colleges', which are sometimes independent and sometimes attached to affiliated colleges, and its control vests with the university. In Madhya Pradesh, where all secondary schools have been raised to the higher secondary pattern, there is no course at this stage outside the higher secondary schools. In States where the higher secondary pattern is adopted but all high schools have not been raised to the higher secondary status, the stage is provided as class XI in the higher secondary schools and pre-university courses in colleges. All other States provide a pre-university course exclusively located in colleges and controlled by the universities.

Transfer of Pre-University Course

The Commission attach great significance to the location, exclusively in the schools, of all the courses that form part of higher secondary education. When the higher secondary pattern was first recommended, the pre-university course was introduced only as a transitional measure.

Unfortunately, the transition threatens to become permanent, and even today about 40 per cent of the total enrolment in the universities and affiliated colleges is in the intermediate or pre-university courses. This is a great evil from all points of view. It is bad for the universities and colleges as their resources and energies are being improperly utilized and even wasted in doing what is essentially the work of secondary schools. It is bad for the secondary schools because they are weakened by being deprived of a stage which could give them good teachers and facilities, with the result that they are obliged to do a good deal of work which ought to have been done at the primary stage.

It is bad for the students because they are now required to enter universities at too early an age, and compelled to learn through methods of higher education which are beyond their capacity and more suited to maturer students. We, therefore, strongly recommend that the pre-university course, irrespective of its duration, should first be transferred to the school on a high priority basis-this transfer to be completed by the end of the Fifth Five Year Plan at the latest.

The following measures may be adopted to bring about this transfer:

(1) The responsibility for transferring all pre-university or intermediate work from the universities and affiliated colleges should be placed on the University Grants Commission, which should be asked to prepare a phased programme, to be spread over not more than ten years, for the purpose. A beginning should be made with the universities and the postgraduate colleges which should be required to shed this work as soon as practicable. This policy should then be extended to degree colleges, where the enrolments at this stage should be frozen at a certain time, after which the colleges would be required to taper them off as their enrolments at the undergraduate stage begin to grow. Beyond the Fourth Plan, the opening of new pre-university or intermediate classes in the universities and affiliated colleges should not be permitted. The University Grants Commission and the State Governments should be requested to reduce gradually their allotment of funds earmarked for this stage of education and to stop them completely by the end of the Fifth Plan.

(2) While these steps are being taken, arrangements should be made to start the higher secondary class or classes in selected schools. The responsibility for making these arrangements should be placed on the State Education Departments, which should work out a proper programme for the purpose in consultation with the universities in the State. Good high schools should be selected and given adequate grant-in-aid to start a higher secondary class or classes as a self-contained unit which is not to be integrated with the lower classes, so that students from other high schools may join it. A scheme of this type has been tried in Mysore and found to work well. Recurring grants for this purpose should be

made available to each selected institution one year in advance so that the preliminary arrangements can be satisfactorily completed in time.

(3) Most of the Boards of Secondary Education will have to be reconstituted to accept the responsibility for the higher secondary stage, and in some cases, their Acts will have to be amended.

This programme of transfer will not involve any wastage. The universities and the affiliated colleges from which the preuniversity courses will disappear will be able to utilize the existing facilities so released for the purpose of expanded admissions in undergraduate classes. For creating the new facilities required at the school stage, however, a much larger investment of resources is needed. The nonrecurring expenditure will be much greater, because most of the secondary schools are in a very bad shape at present. Even with regard to recurring expenditure, there will be an overall increase, because the income from fees may show a fall after a transfer of these classes to the schools. But the advantage of this additional investment Will be spread, to some extent, over a very large proportion of the student population at the secondary stage and the benefit to society in terms of a better output from secondary education, will be much greater. There should, therefore, be no hesitation in incurring the somewhat larger expenditure involved in the execution of this programme.

Programme for Lengthening of Duration

The Kothari commission recommended that in all the States except Uttar Pradesh and Kerala, the duration of the higher secondary course should be lengthened to two years through a phased programme spread over twenty years and divided into two stages. The first stage, covering a period of five years, should be devoted to securing a better utilization of existing facilities and to making the needed preparation for a successful implementation of this important reform. Even during this period, selected higher secondary schools should be permitted to add the twelfth year, and some high schools of good quality and possessing the necessary facilities may be allowed to introduce the two-year higher secondary course as pilot projects. The second stage will cover a span of fifteen years; the programme of extending the duration should begin in the Fifth Plan, gather momentum in the following decade, and be completed by the end of the Seventh Plan.

The Commission recommend such postponement for three important reasons:

(1) The first reason is that of priority. There are three possible choices in school or higher education in the next five years: qualitative improvement of general education (with special emphasis on raising the salaries and qualifications of teachers); vocationalization of secondary and higher education; or lengthening of the duration of the total period of general education.

(2) The second reason is our anxiety for improving the utilization of the time already available before the duration of the school course is lengthened. The Commission emphasized that a hasty addition of one year to secondary education will not lead to qualitative improvement unless there is a proper climate of hard work in the educational institutions. Moreover, 'time' is only one of the 'inputs' that can bring about improvement in quality. There are several other 'inputs' that are necessary for raising standards, e.g., motivation of students, competence of teachers, upgraded curricula, better methods of teaching and evaluation, improved textbooks and teaching materials and adequate equipment,

buildings and other physical facilities. Qualitative improvement will result from the cumulative effect of all these factors. If they are of the right kind, an increase in the duration will certainly add to the improvement in quality; but if they are not, the extension of the course by a year may only mean further wastage.

(3) The third reason is related to the need to make advance preparation for the lengthening of the duration. According to the Commission, it will be nothing short of wasting scarce resources if State Governments embark on this programme without preparatory work. This requires (a) that State Governments should take the necessary steps, right from the moment the proposal is accepted, to expand postgraduate education and to prepare the needed teachers; and (b) that they should select, by way of a pilot project, good secondary or higher secondary schools and permit them to add two or one-year courses, as the case may be. On the completion of these courses, the students should be able to join the undergraduate courses at the appropriate points. This will be broadly equivalent to the 'advance placement programme in the USA. It will be of considerable help to several students who would prefer to work for some time longer with their own school teachers and in their own school atmosphere rather than transfer themselves abruptly to a new and unfamiliar environment.

In this connection, it is 'interesting to note that the Committee on Higher Education in the United Kingdom, after considering a somewhat similar suggestion for lengthening the duration of the first degree course in the United Kingdom from three to four years, turned it down principally on the ground that a general extension of the course would not be justified while students were not making proper use of the vacations. This reinforces the view that the proper policy to be adopted in this matter, especially in a developing country, is to increase the duration only after all steps have been taken to maximize the utilization of the time available.

Vocationalization at the Higher Secondary Stage

A large variety of terminal courses should be organized, varying in duration from one to three years. They will include courses for the training of primary and preprimary teachers; courses conducted by the industrial training institutions for a large number of trades for which the completion of studies in class X is the minimum qualification; courses in agriculture and industry which will train the middle level of personnel needed; courses for training paramedical/health personnel; courses for secretariat work; and courses in home science. It is such courses that will make secondary education mainly terminal. The problem is discussed in detail elsewhere.

The Kothari Commission recommend that:

(1) the higher secondary stage should be extended to cover a period of two years and should be located exclusively in the schools;

(2) steps should be taken to implement this reform through a phased programme spread over the next 20 years (1966-85);

(3) as a first step in this direction, the pre-university course, irresPective of its duration, should be transferred from the colleges to the schools on a high priority basis within the next ten years;

(4) simultaneously, attempts should be made in the Fourth Five Year Plan for improving the utilization of the existing period to the best extent possible, for the preparation of teachers for the two-year course

by expanding and improving the postgraduate stage, and for the working out of pilot projects with two-year higher secondary courses in selected secondary schools;

(5) with the beginning of the Fifth Five Year Plan (197172), the implementation of the programme should start on a large scale and it should be completed by the end of the Seventh Plan (1985-86); and

(6) provision should also be made from the very outset for the introduction of different types of vocational courses at the higher secondary stage, varying in duration from one to three years, which would prepare young persons for employment.

Reorganisation at Universal Stage

Prior to 1947, the pattern of higher education was largely uniform in all parts of the country. The duration of the course leading to the first degree in arts and science was two years, and this was followed by a two-year course leading to the second degree. But several changes have been introduced into the pattern since Independence. The most important is that the duration of the course for the first degree in arts, science and commerce has been lengthened to three years in all the universities except those in Uttar Pradesh and the University of Bombay, which still provide the two-year degree course after the Intermediate Examination. One or two universities have experimented with an honours course in certain subjects, covering a period of four years in the aggregate. Again, the degree courses in professional subjects are generally longer than the courses for the degrees in arts and science. The agricultural and the engineering courses extend to four and five years respectively after the preuniversity course, and the medical course has an even longer duration.

Proposals for Reorganization

Since progress in higher education lies through freedom to experiment, there can be no objection to this variety. The principal criticism of higher education is directed, however, not so much against the pattern of organization as against the comparatively low standards of the degrees awarded by the Indian universities in arts, commerce and science.

The Kothari commission made the following proposals with the question of the structural reorganization necessary at the university stage for the improvement of standards.

(1) The duration of the first degree course should not be less than three years. Apart from this, there should be no rigidity about the duration of courses in higher education. These may vary from university to university, and even in the same university, from subject to subject. The duration of courses for the second degree may be two or three years.

(2) In some universities, strong 'graduate schools' providing a three-year M.A./M.Sc./M.Com. degree course may be established in certain subjects. For the sake of convenience, these courses may be designated as honours courses or they may be given some other suitable name. If they are properly organized and a careful selection of students is made, they Will be able to produce excellent personnel for the teaching faculty and for high-grade research.

(3) A beginning should also be made with the organization of four-year special courses for the first degree in selected subjects. The first year of these courses will be the same as the first year of the present three-year degree course. But students will be selected, at the end of that year, for admission to

a further three-year special course leading to the first (special) degree in, the subject. The experiment should be tried, in the first instance, in the university departments only and in subjects where teachers and facilities are available. In the light of the experience gained, it may be extended subsequently to other subjects and to good affiliated colleges doing postgraduate work.

(4) The above proposal will need to be modified in Uttar Pradesh, where the immediate problem is to raise the duration of the first degree course in arts, commerce and science from two to three years.

(5) Suitable 'bridges' should be built between these new and longer courses and the existing courses of shorter duration.

(6) Some incentives will have to be provided to students for undergoing these longer and higher level courses. For instance, a more liberal provision of scholarships should be made for these longer courses for the first and the second degrees. Students completing the courses should be entitled to advance increments in the usual scales. They should receive preferential consideration in recruitment; and as soon as the supply becomes adequate, the recruitment of teachers should be restricted to the holders of these degrees only. It need hardly be stressed that the admissions to these courses should be made on a highly selective basis.

Utilization or Facilities

The principal object of the changes in structure and duration which have been discussed above is to raise standards. In this context, however, it is essential to note that

— structure and duration play a significant but secondary role in improving standards;

— the changes proposed in structure and duration will be rather slow in making an impact on quality, because their full implementation has been spread over twenty years; and

— the most serious weakness of the existing educational system lies, not in its structure, but in its feebleness.

It will be generally agreed that the facilities in our educational system, deficient as they are, are not utilized to their full advantage. There is much that can be done to improve standards even in existing circumstances by lengthening the school day, increasing the number of working days, making full use of the long vacations, and generally creating a climate of hard and sustained work. The key to rapid national development is dedication and hard work. Educational institutions should give a lead to society in this matter and create the required climate, in the first instance, in the educational system itself.

Working and Instructional Days

At present, the total number of working days and hours prescribed for educational institutions at all levels is inadequate. What is far worse, a very large proportion of these working days is lost to education for a variety of reasons with the result that the total number of instructional days, i.e., days which are fully utilized for instructional purposes, is often reduced to an absurdly low figure. The details of a study conducted by the Commission to ascertain the number of working days and hours in schools and colleges in different parts of the country (as officially prescribed by the State Education Departments and universities) has been given elsewhere. It shows that there is considerable variation, from area to area, in the total number of working days in a year-these range from 172 to 309 at the school stage and from 120 to 240 at the university stage. The number of holidays given within a school year shows even larger variations- from 20 to 75 at the school stage and from 4 to 49 at the university stage. Similarly, the total duration of vacations varies from 36 to 84 days at the school stage and from 62 to 137 at the university stage. The days utilized for examinations (inclusive of preparatory leave) vary from 10 to 77 and the loss on account of celebrations such as foundation days, annual functions of societies, etc is sometimes as high as 40 to 60 days in a year. These facts are a sad reflection on the efficiency of the educational system, and the general under- utilization which they represent in a developing economy like ours is tantamount to an unpardonable waste of scarce resources. We, therefore, recommend that the number of instructional days in a year should be increased to about 234 (or 39 weeks) for schools and 216 (or 36 weeks) for colleges (and pre-primary schools).

Utilization of Vacations. In addition, steps should be taken to ensure that adequate use is made of vacations which are very often wasted. Even in advanced countries, where vacations are already being utilized much better than here, there is a growing feeling that they could be used even more intensively. A country like India cannot afford to waste vacation time.

It is quite possible to organize interesting and challenging programmes for students, such as

— participation in social service camps, NCC and workexperience;
— earning for maintenance;
— studies for the ensuing year, including general studies, with the help of school and college libraries and laboratories;
— hikes, excursions, tours, cultivation of bobbies; and
— participation in nation-building programmes such as literacy drives.

For these programmes, it will be essential to secure the assistance of a certain proportion of teachers. This could be done by the appointment of additional staff, by the payment of honorarium at prescribed rates to the existing staff, or by granting them compensatory leave in lieu of the vacation lost.

School Hours

It is not enough simply to increase the number of instructional days. For the best results, it is also essential to increase the duration of the working day as indicated below:

(1) At the school stage, the working hours per day should vary from four hours at the pre-primary stage to about six hours at the higher secondary stage. This total period does not include the time for co-curricular activities, but includes the time when the students would be working on their own (e.g., the library period), or on guided studies. In an academic year, the hours of instruction at the lower primary stage should be about 900, and at the higher primary and secondary stages, they should be not less than 1,000, and preferably raised to 1,100 or even 1,200 if conditions are favourable.

(2) At the university stage, the hours of work are already long enough for professional courses (e.g., engineering, medicine, agriculture) and also for science students. It is only the students in the humanities courses who do not seem to work hard enough. The more serious weakness of the situation, however, is the lack of adequate facilities for students to study on their own.

According to Kothari commission, the 'contact' hours at this stage should be about 15 to 20 a week; but that they should involve the student in working on his own for at least twice as much, so that his total work-load per week is about 50 to 60 hours. As one goes higher up, the contact hours could be less, and self-study periods even longer. At present, students and teachers come together in lectures, where there is hardly any personal contact, and there is no other way in which they can meet. The most urgent reform needed, therefore, is not to lengthen the working day in terms of the lectures delivered- these need to be cut down-but to increase the self-study facilities for students and to ensure that they work adequately. To make it possible, several additional facilities, now lacking in most of our educational institutions, will have to be provided. A well-kept and commodious library with an adequate number of 'reading seats' is necessary; teachers must have rooms, or, lacking this, separate desks of their own in the library; and canteens should be established to provide substantial meals prepared at a reasonable cost under hygienic conditions for students and teachers. Owing mainly to the financial implications involved, it may not be possible to adopt this reform in all institutions.

Utilization of Institutional Facilities

One more aspect of the problem needs attention. Since it is very costly to provide and maintain the physical plant of educational institutions, it becomes necessary to utilize it as fully as possible, for the longest time on each day and for all the days in the year, by making suitable administrative arrangements. Teachers and students would continue to have their own hours of work and vacations as recommended above. The libraries, laboratories, workshops, craftsheds, etc., should be open all the year round and should be utilized for at least eight hours a day, if not longer. Special vacation programmes should be arranged to utilize institutional facilities for community service, adult education, temporary hostels for day students, enrichment programmes for gifted students and supporting programmes for retarded students. It is not necessary to indicate all the different ways in which the institutional facilities could be utilized all the year round. If an understanding is developed that educational institutions are like temples of learning and should never remain closed, and if a proper climate for sustained work is created, teachers, students and the local communities will themselves discover innumerable methods of utilizing school facilities to the maximum potential throughout the year. As it is difficult to expand educational facilities adequately and wasteful to under-utilize existing resources, such programmes demand urgent attention.

EVOLVING STANDARDS

One of the common criticisms against the development of education in the post-Independence period is that there has been a fall in standards, and two main illustrations are given to support it: the increase in the number of sub-standard institutions of general education, and the increase in the number of students with sub- standard attainments. The first of these is far more serious and is largely the cause of the second. There is considerable force in this criticism and we do not wish to minimize its gravity. But we would not like to ignore the other side of the picture either. It has to be remembered that

— a part of the increase in the number of students with 'sub-standard' attainments is due to the first generation learners, who depress the standards to some extent, but whose entry into secondary schools and colleges in large numbers, especially in rural areas, is also a sign of progress;
— considerable improvements have been made in recent years in the teaching of several subjects;

— good institutions and first-rate students are now more numerous and qualitatively as good as ever, if not better; and

— the total amount of education in society is substantially higher at present than at any time in the past. The overall situation is thus a mixed picture of light and shade, of improvement as well as deterioration, and of a rise in standards in some areas accompanied by a comparative decline in others. While we fully support the need and urgency for raising standards, we would also like to recognize the qualitative achievements of the educational system in the last few years.

Criteria for Evaluating Standards

The basic issue in educational reconstruction is not to compare the standards of today with those of the past or to determine whether they are rising or falling. On the other hand, we should judge them on the basis of three interrelated criteria: adequacy, dynamism, and international comparability. Standards must be:

— adequate in relation to the tasks for which they are intended;

— dynamic, and should keep on rising with the demands for the higher levels of knowledge, skills or character which a modernizing society makes; and

— internationally comparable, at least in those key sectors where such comparison is important.

A lower standard for these degrees was deliberately adopted in the early years of higher education, because universities had to institute a quick first degree in arts and science in order to produce the large number of graduates needed for the expanding administration. The weakness of these degrees was pointed out by the Calcutta University Commission more than forty years ago. But the situation has not materially changed to this day. Meanwhile, advanced countries have made phenomenal progress in education, specially since the Second World War. The gap between our standards and theirs has widened further; and the holders of the first degree of our universities in arts and science are now generally equated with matriculates in the important universities of western countries and are eligible for admisSion only to the first year of their first degree course.

The Kothari Commission recommend that an intensive effort should be made, through measures for reorganization of the structure, increase of duration, intensive utilization and improvement of the quality and extent of inputs other than time, to raise standards continually at all stages of education. The immediate programmes to be undertaken from this point of view should be the following:

1) Standards at the End of the First Stage of School Education. The standards reached at the end of the first ten years of school education. at present are far from satisfactory. We, therefore, recommend that for the next ten years the principal effort ill all the States and Union Territories should be directed towards the qualitative improvement of this stage of school education so that its wastage-which reaches appalling dimensions at present-is reduced to the minimum.

2) Standards at the University Stage. Beyond Class X, the commission have proposed the addition of at least one year of time. If we intensify utilization and improve other inputs, it may be possible to add a year of content to this stage also. The total gain would thus be equal to two years of content and this would raise the standards of our degrees considerably. When the standard at the end of the

> first stage of school education is raised by one year of content, the standards of our degrees will rise even higher. Against this background, with the adoption of the programme of developing a few major universities which we shall discuss elsewhere, we could make the standards of some of our universities comparable to the best institutions of their type in any part of the world.

The Commission have referred earlier to the popular misconception that it is essential to have a uniform pattern of school and higher education in order to improve or maintain standards. But while we are opposed to uniformity of pattern, we do very much share the general concern over the necessity for a continual improvement of standards and their comparability between different parts of the country. According to the Commission, this objective can be better secured at the school stage through the creation of an adequate and efficient machinery at the State and the national levels, for defining, revising and evaluating national standards at the end of the primary, high school and the higher secondary stages.

Still another way in which standards can be raised is by securing better coordination between the different stages of education and by making the educational institutions function in small groups instead of in isolation. At present, there is little practical coordination between educational institutions functioning at different levels of education. The people at the university stage criticize those at the secondary stage for a fall in standards; and those at the secondary stage pass the blame on to the persons at the primary stage. This situation of mutual recrimination has to be changed into one of mutual help, and this can be done by making each higher stage of education take the responsibility for improving standards at the lower stages.

Role of Universities and Colleges

The universities and colleges, for example, should assist the secondary schools in improving their efficiency. The following are some of the programmes which can be undertaken:

— Each college can be functionally related to a number of secondary schools in the neighbourhood and enabled to provide extension services and guidance to them to improve their standards. A similar programme for the colleges themselves could be developed through the universities.

— The universities can conduct special diploma courses, either pre-service or in-service, for improving the competence of secondary teachers. These can preferably be correspondence courses, requiring only short-term personal attendance.

— The universities can conduct experimental secondary or primary schools to evolve improved techniques of teaching and organization.

— The university and college teachers can take upon themselves the responsibility for improving school textbooks and providing better types of instructional materials.

— The universities and colleges could select talented students from the schools in different subjects at an appropriate stage, say, in the age-group 13-15, and help them to develop their knowledge in special fields through individual guidance, provision of laboratory facilities, etc., over and above regular school work.

These programmes have been cited merely as illustrations. Once the principle that the universities should assist in the improvement of standards at lower stages is accepted, it will be possible to devise many other programmes.

The School Complex

What was stated above for the relationship between universities, colleges and secondary schools, could be easily extended further to secondary and primary schools. There are about 26,000 secondary schools at the beginning of the Fourth Plan and about 14,000 of these are in rural areas. In addition, the rural areas have about 65,000 higher primary schools and about 360,000 lower primary schools. In other words, in a rural area having a radius of five to ten miles, there are: one secondary school, about five higher primary schools and 28 lower primary schools. The total number of teachers may be about 80 to 100. This is a fairly small and manageable group which can function in a face-to-face relationship within easily accessible distance. It has also a good potential for planning and guidance, since there will be at least five or six trained graduates in the group. Moreover, it is possible to provide new aids like a projector, a good library, a good laboratory in each secondary school as a unit and make them functionally available to all the schools in the area. This group built round a secondary school should, according to the Commission, be adopted as the minimum viable unit of educational reform and developed accordingly.

The linking of secondary and primary schools under this programme can be done in two tiers. In the first tier, each higher primary school should be integrally related to the eight to ten lower primary schools that exist in its neighbourhood so that they form one complex' of educational facilities. The headmaster of the higher primary school should provide an extension service to the lower primary schools in his charge, and it will be his responsibility to see that they function properly. For this purpose, there would be a committee under his chairmanship (of which the headmaster of every lower primary school in his area would be a member) which would be responsible for planning and developing all the schools as a single 'complex'. The second tier would be a committee under the chairmanship of the headmaster of the secondary school (all headmasters of the higher and lower primary schools in the area being members) which will plan the work and give guidance to all the schools in the area, in the light of which each higher primary school complex (with its associated lower primary schools) would carry on its work. This group of schools and teachers can be given a good deal of freedom to develop their own programmes, subject to the general guidance of the inspecting staff. The group should also be requested to coordinate its work with the local communities and to derive as much help from this source as possible.

Such an organization will have several advantages in helping to promote educational advance. It will break the terrible isolation under which each school functions at present. It will enable a small group of schools working in a neighbourhood to make a cooperative effort to improve standards. It will enable the Education Department to devolve authority with comparatively less fear of its being misused and to provide the necessary stock of talent at the functional level to make use of this freedom.

Three Channels of Education

One of the major weaknesses of the existing educational system is that it places an almost exclusive reliance on full-time instruction and does not develop adequately the two alternative channels of part-time education and private study or own-time education. It has to be remembered that reliance on fulltime education as the sole channel of instruction often divides the life of an individual into three water-tight and sharply divided stages: a pre-school stage of no formal education or work, a school stage of full-time education and no work, and a post-school stage of full-time work and no education. in a modernizing and rapidly changing society, education should be regarded, not as a terminal but as a life-long process. It should begin informally in the home itself; and thereafter, it should be the ultimate objective of national policy to strive to bring every Individual under the influence of the formal system of education as early as possible, and to keep him under it, directly or indirectly, throughout his life. Similarly, there should be no water-tight separation between work and education at any stave of a man's life, but only a relative shift of emphasis. An 'individual under full-time education should have some work-experience as an integral part of his education itself; and every full-time worker should have the inclination, leisure and means of continuing his education still further. In the same way, the transition from one stage to another should not be abrupt. For example, the transfer of an individual from the infant's play-dominated world to formal school should include a transitional phase of gentle preparation and orientation to schooling. A young person should not be compelled to pass abruptly from a stage of full-time education to another of full-time work; it would be desirable to interpose a period of part-time education and part-time work between the two.

If these objectives are to be attained, it is necessary to abandon the present policy of placing an almost exclusive reliance on full-time education, and the two alternative channels of part-time and own-time education should be developed on a larger scale at every stage and in every sector of education and should be given the same status as fulltime education. Secondly, adult and continuing education, which is almost totally neglected at present, should be emphasized to a very great extent. Taken together, these two reforms would

— enable those who have not completed a stage of education to complete it and, if they wish, to proceed to the next;

— help every educated person to have further education with or without formally enrolling himself in an educational institution.;

— enable a worker to acquire knowledge, ability and vocational skill in order to be a better worker and to improve his chances of earning more; and

— help to refresh the knowledge of the educated person and enable him to keep pace with the new knowledge in the field of his interest.

Programmes of this type, which are being developed even in educationally advanced and affluent countries, cannot be ignored in an underdeveloped and poor country like India. They will smoothen the transition from school to life, reduce the cost of education to the State, and bring under the influence of the educational system a large number of persons who desire to educate themselves but cannot do so on economic grounds.

5

Recommendations for Teacher Development

Of all the different factors which influence the quality of education and its contribution to national development, the quality,competence and character of teachers are undoubtedly the most significant. Nothing is more important than securing a sufficient supply of high quality recruits to the teaching profession, providing them with the best possible professions preparation and creating satisfactory conditions of work in which they can be fully effective. In view of the rapid expansion of educational facilities expected during the next three Plans, and specially in view of the urgent need to raise standards to the highest level and to keep them continually improving, these problems have now acquired unprecedented importance and urgency.

A programme of high priority in the proposed educational reconstruction, therefore, is to feed back a significant proportion of the talented men and women from schools and colleges into the educational system. For this purpose, it is necessary to make an intensive and continuous effort to raise the economic, social and professional status of teachers in order to attract young men and women of ability to the profession, and to retain them in it as dedicated, enthusiastic and contented workers. This can be done, to a very limited extent only, through appealing to motives such as love of children or of teaching, interest in academic work or research, idealism and desire for social service, which attract a small proportion of able young: persons to the teaching profession. There can, however, be no doubt that the provision of adequate remuneration, opportunities for professional advancement and favourable conditions of service and work, are the major programmes which will help to initiate and maintain this 'feedback' process.

Remuneration

In the post-Independence period, continuous efforts have been made to improve the remuneration of teachers at all levels and schemes for this purpose have figured prominently in all the Plans. But the net results achieved have not been adequate, particularly in respect of primary school teachers.

It will be seen that the increase in the remuneration of the different categories of teachers is far from uniform. The largest proportional increase has taken place in the salaries of teachers in primary schools. But owing to the very low levels of remuneration which obtained in 1950-51, these are still far from satisfactory. The improvement in the salaries of teachers in the universities, vocation- al schools and colleges is also noticeable. But in the colleges of arts and science and in secondary schools, there has been an actual decrease in remuneration in real terms. The picture is worst at the pre-primary stage because the salaries in pre-primary schools are governed, not so much by departmental regulations, as by market conditions. This is because most of the pre-school institutions are unaided and located in urban areas where an over-abundant supply of women teachers is available.

It will also be noted that a good deal of the effect of the increase in remuneration at all stages has been offset by the rise in the cost of living which has taken place during this period-the remunerations in the various types of institutions have risen by 18 to 92 per cent while the cost of living has risen by 65 per cent. It is only in four types of institutions-vocational schools (69 per cent), universities (73 per cent), higher primary schools (80 per cent) and lower primary schools (92 per cent) that the rise in remuneration has exceeded that in the cost of living. In some sectors, e.g., pre- primary, the increase in the cost of living has been greater than that in remuneration. On the whole, there was some improvement in the remuneration of teachers in real terms up to 1960-61. This has since been almost completely neutralized by the sharp increase in prices that has taken place in the last two or three years.

The Commission made a study of the remuneration of teachers in all the States and Union Territories. It revealed two major weaknesses:

(1) Inter-State Differences. There are substantial differences in the remuneration of teachers from State to State, particularly at the school stage; and

(2) Intra-State Differences. Even within a State, there are variations in remuneration. At the university stage, salaries vary from faculty to faculty. The teachers in affiliated colleges do not have the same scales of pay as those in universities. At the school stage, there are often substantial differences in the remuneration of teachers working in institutions under different managements.

There has been a strong demand for the abolition of these variations. It has been suggested that the first type of variation can be eliminated or reduced to the minimum by adopting national scales of pay with adjustment in allowances for inevitable local variations in the cost of living and that the second should be offset by adopting the principle of parity. Both these proposals need a closer examination.

National Scales of Pay

The demand for the introduction of national scales of pay for all categories of teachers is supported unanimously by teachers' organizations. The proposal had a ready acceptance in higher education because of the developments in the post-Independence period. The University Education Commission recommended that the multiplicity of scales of pay which then existed in the universities and colleges Should be reduced to the minimum and that an attempt should be made to adopt national scales of pay for teachers in higher education. This recommendation was broadly accepted and some action to implement it has since been taken. The UGC is attempting to introduce common scales of pay for different categories of teachers in the universities and similar scales of pay for teachers in affiliated colleges. Attempts for the 'introduction of common scales of pay are also being made, with a fair amount of success, in respect of engineering institutions. It is true that, in spite of all that has been done during the last ten years, there are still considerable variations in the scales of pay of teachers in higher education. But the important point is that the general princi- ple of adopting national scales of pay has been broadly accepted; and all that is needed is to make a more determined effort to move forward on the lines already set. This is a comparatively simpler issue.

At the school stage, however, the problem is more difficult because the desirability of introducing national scales of pay at this stage is itself challenged. It is argued, for instance, that as the cost of living varies from one part of the country to another, a common national scale of pay would really imply unequal payment and cause considerable hardship to school teachers with lower levels of 'income. It is also pointed out that the supply and demand position for the different categories of teachers varies considerably from one part of the country to another. Women teachers, for instance, are readily available in some areas and are very difficult to obtain in others. Under these circumstances, it is pointed out that a common scale of pay would make it more difficult to recruit them in just those areas where they are most needed. There is some force in these arguments. They only make out a case for providing local allowances in addition to basic national scales of pay rather than disprove the need to adopt minimum national scales of pay to reduce the large disparities that now exist in the salaries of school teachers in different States. We, therefore, recommended that, at the school stage, the Government of India should lay down the minimum scales of pay for school teachers. The States and Union Territories should then adopt equivalent or higher scales of pay to suit their local conditions.

The Principle of Parity' With regard to the intra-State differences, the commission recommended that the remuneration of teachers working under different managements should also be the same and that all teachers having the same qualifications and the same responsibilities should have the same, or at least similar, remuneration and conditions of work and service. The problem will have to be discussed separately for higher and school education.

(1) *Higher Education.* There is a good deal of disparity in the remuneration of teachers of different categories in higher education. For instance, the remuneration of teachers in different faculties is not the same: the teachers in the faculties of engineering and medicine are paid higher than those in the humanities. There is also a difference, in most parts of the country, between the salaries given to teachers in universities

and those given to teachers in affiliated colleges. In many States, teachers in government colleges do not get the scales of pay given to university teachers, although their remuneration is often much better than that of teachers in affiliated colleges. The commission recommended that these differences should be reduced to the minimum and efforts made to eliminate them gradually.

(2) *School Teachers*. The Kothari commission recommended that the scales of pay of school teachers belonging to the same category but working under different managements such as government, local bodies or private organizations, should be the same. The existing variations are purely historical in origin. The administrative authorities under the British did not wish to reduce the salaries of government servants; at the same time, they were anxious to keep salary costs down to a level which the economy could afford. Hence the salaries 'of teachers in local authority schools were deliberately fixed at a point lower than that for government teachers and those for teachers in private schools were fixed at a still lower point. This policy has had two unfortunate results: it has lowered the average wage for teachers in general, as teachers in government service were a very small minority; it has also introduced an undesirable 'caste' system among them. It is time to eliminate these relics of the past.

A move in this direction has already been initiated and is well on the way. The principle of parity has been accepted at all levels of school education in seven States (Andhra Pradesh, Kerala, Madhya Pradesh, Madras, Mysore, Punjab and Rajasthan). In three States (Assam, Gujarat and Maharashtra) it has been accepted at the primary level, but not at the secondary for all categories of teachers. In five States (Bihar, Jammu and Kashmir,

Orissa, Uttar Pradesh and West Bengal) it has not been accepted at any stage and the scales of pay prescribed for teachers in non-government schools are different and much lower. It will be seen that, in some cases, the differences are marginal while in others, they are serious and glaring.

Three main arguments are put forward for retaining this disparity in remuneration. The first is that the teachers in non-government schools are not well-qualified and not properly selected. Instead of perpetuating unequal remuneration on these grounds, it is essential to adopt the principle of parity in remuneration, and simultaneously to prescribe the same qualifications for teachers in all types of schools and to introduce a similar machinery for their recruitment. The second is that teachers in government service have certain handicaps such as liability to transfer, application of conduct and discipline rules, etc., and that parity in remuneration would tilt the balance materially in favour of teachers in private schools.

There are bound to be some differences in conditions of service in government and non-government institutions. For instance, private educational institutions call provide a more satisfying experience to certain persons while teachers in government schools have better prospects of promotion. But in the proposals formulated by us, these differences have been reduced to the minimum and there is, therefore, no justification to continue the existing disparity of remuneration. The third argument put forward is financial and it is said that the funds needed to upgrade the salaries of teachers in local authority and private schools to the level of those in government schools are not readily available.

Revision of Salaries

In making thier proposals for the revision of the

remuneration of teachers, The Kothari commission have kept the following principles in view:

(1) *At the university stage,* the remuneration of teachers should be broadly comparable with that of the senior services of the Government so that a fair proportion of the top talent in the country is attracted to the profession of teaching and research. What is important here is that the salary of a vice-chancellor should be about the same as that of a Secretary to the Union Government; the maximum salary of a university professor should be the same as the maximum in the senior scale of the IAS; and for outstanding professors, higher salaries comparable to super-time scales of pay of the IAS should be available.

(2) The scales of pay of primary teachers should be comparable to those of public servants with similar qualifications and responsibilities. But they should have a higher basic pay in recognition of the two years of professional training which they have received.

(3) Since teaching is a unified profession, requiring common attitudes of devotion and dedication and since teachers at every stage are entrusted with the responsibility of educating the younger generation, the differences in the remuneration of the teachers at the different levels-primary, secondary and university-should be reduced to the minimum. For example, the minimum salaries of primary, secondary and university teachers should be in the ratio of 1 : 2 : 3. At present, the starting salary of a primary teacher can be as low as Rs. 60-80, which is about one-twelfth to one-sixteenth of the starting salary of a professor.

(4) In order to induce better qualified teachers to teach at the lower stages-the raising of educational standards will ultimately depend upon this-it is essential to adopt a policy under which the scales of pay of teachers at the school stage will be based only on qualifications and be made independent of the sub- stage-pre-primary, lower primary, higher primary, lower secondary or higher secondary-in which-they might be serving. While the commission accepted this idea in principle, it may not be possible, on financial grounds, to adopt it immediately in toto. However, the commission has taken the view that at least the headmas- ters of all large lower primary schools (say, with an enrol- ment of about 200) and of all higher primary schools should be trained graduates and should have the same scale of pay as that of trained graduate teachers in secondary schools. Similarly, a certain proportion of the teachers at the sec- ondary stage should have the same qualifications and the same scales of pay as those of junior lecturers in affiliated colleges.

(5) The improvement in salary scales should not be entirely automatic: it should be linked with the improvement in quali- fications and quality.

Salaries of Teachers

In the light of these general principles, the commission proposed the following scales of pay:

Reform at the University Stage

As a result of the recom- mendations of the University Education Commission and the work done by the UGC during the last ten years, considerable improvement has been made in regard to the scales of pay of teachers at the university stage. The multiplicity of scales which existed in the past has been reduced and the new scales adopted are more comparable to those in the senior administrative services of the Government of India.

National scales of pay have been suggested for teachers in universities and in affiliated colleges and these are being increasingly adopted by the institutions concerned. The Kothari commission also welcome the recent decision of the Government of India, on the recommendation of the UGC, to sanction the new scales of pay for university teachers which have been indicated above. The main points to be considered in this context, therefore, are two: (a) implementation of these proposals; and (b) relating them to improvement in quality and qualifications of teachers.

To facilitate the introduction of these scales at an early date, and especially in private institutions which are so numerous, the Kothari commission recommended that assistance from the Centre be provided to meet the additional expenditure on a sharing basis of 80 per cent from the Central funds and 20 per cent by the State Government and that, in the case of private colleges, the Central assistance may even be provided on a 100 per cent basis. Such assistance should continue during the Fourth Plan period; and, in the meanwhile, steps may be taken by the State Governments to devise an appropriate system of grant-in-aid for placing the revised scales on a permanent basis.

(1) Teachers in Universities. In regard to the qualifications and selection procedures for university teachers, the commission agree with the recommendations made by the Model Act Committee which it quote for ready reference:

The standard and quality of work of a university depends very largely on the quality of its teachers. It is most important that every care is exercised by the authorities concerned so that teachers of the highest competency are recruited by the universities. Also the conditions of service and opportunities for professional advancement should be such as would attract and retain in the service of the universities men of outstanding ability. The power to appoint teachers must be vested in the Executive Council, but all the teaching appointments should be made by the Executive Council only on the recommendation of a properly constituted Selection Committee. The Selection Committee should consist, besides the Vice-Chancellor and the Head of the Department concerned, of a certain number of experts. This number may vary in accordance with the category of teachers to be appointed. For a professor, it should be necessary to have two or even three outside experts. It may be an advantage to have one nominee of the Chancellor/Visitor on the Selection Committee. The Court or the Academic Council should not select a representative to the Selection Committee. It should be a clear rule that the Executive Council should accept the selection unanimously recommended by the Selection Committee. In rare cases, if for good reasons the Executive Council is unable to accept the recommendation of the Selection Committee, efforts for a better selection may be renewed in the following year. A great deal of what is described as university politics or interference of outside politics in universities arises in connection with appointments. Universities must have the freedom to make their own appointments; but they must be steadfast in their desire to make right appointments.

(2) The commission's attention has been drawn to the fact that, in most universities, candidates for

appointment as professors are called for interview before a selection committee. Each candidate is interviewed by the committee for 10 to 15 minutes. In the case of such high level appointments, interviews have hardly any meaning, and, in fact, tend to discourage first-rate men from offering for such appointments. Professors should be persons of standing in the subjects and should be known to the experts by reputation in the fields of their work. It should, therefore, be possible for a selection committee to make a selection on the basis of a careful consideration of the information supplied by the candidates and other relevant data which may be available to the committee. If considered necessary, candidates who have been found suitable for appointment by the selection committee may be invited by the vice- chancellor for a personal discussion before making a formal offer of appointment.

(3) Teachers in Affiliated Colleges. The procedure described above will also apply to university colleges. Problems do not generally arise with regard to government colleges where recruitment is done through a Public Service Commission. In private affiliated colleges, however, the situation needs considerable improvement on the following lines:

(a) The qualifications of teachers in these colleges should be prescribed by the universities and should be similar to those prescribed in university departments.

(b) Each post should be advertised and selection committees should be formed on the lines recommended above for the universities.

(c) On the advice of the selection committee, the appointment should be made by the managing committee constituted for the college. As recommended by the Model Act Committee, this managing committee should be a compact body consisting of about 10 members. The composition of this body should be prescribed by the university. The principal of the college should be a member of this body and in addition there should be provision for one or more teachers to be on it, preferably by some method of rotation rather than by election. The university should nominate to the governing body two representatives who should normally be teachers of experience.

(d) If any exemption is to be given at all from the possession of the prescribed qualifications, it should not be for more than a year or two. Even when circumstances demand that the exemption should last for a longer period, such exemption given for a temporary period should not lapse into permanent exemption. It is unfair to admit students to a course unless there are qualified teachers.

(e) While the right to make appointments should vest in the colleges, it should be open to the university to withhold 'recognition' of colleges, if persons with high qualifications are rejected without adequate reasons and others with lower qualifications, even though satisfying the minimum requirements, are appointed. In some of these cases this happens because the institution is, either openly or without avowing it, a narrowly denominational institution. In other cases it may just be a case of improper exercise of patronage by the managing body or it may be due to extraneous pressures.

(f) The commission further recommended that it would be desirable to adopt a discriminating approach between one private management and another. Where good standards are maintained and the management has shown its competence to conduct the institution satisfactorily, greater freedom should be given to it in the choice of its teachers. Where the management is not satisfactory, greater control should be exercised.

Pay Scales for School Stage. As compared to higher education the problem of improving the remuneration of teachers at the school stage is more complex and difficult. It is also far more urgent. This urgency has increased because Government has recently sanctioned new scales of pay for teachers in higher education and thus increased the gap, which was already large, between their salaries and those of the school teachers.

The commission's first proposal is that the existing multiplicity of scales of pay should be reduced and that there should be three main scales of pay for school teachers:

(1) A scale of pay for teachers who have completed the secondary course and are trained and who would form the vast bulk of teachers at the primary stage;

(2) A scale of pay for trained graduates who would form a small proportion of teachers at the primary stage but the vast bulk of teachers at the lower secondary stage;

(3) A scale of pay for teachers with postgraduate qualifications who would form a small proportion of teachers at the lower secondary stage, but the bulk of teachers at the higher secondary stage.

Incentives to teachers of special subjects or to teachers with additional qualifications can be given in the form of advance increments or special allowance. The scales of pay of special teachers can also be related to these three basic scales in some suitable manner. The scales of pay for librarians should also be related to those for teachers in a suitable manner.

Scales of Pay of Teachers Who Have Completed the Secondary Course

With regard to this category of teachers, the commission make the following recommendations:

(1) There should be no teacher at the primary stage who has not completed the secondary school course and has not had two years of professional education.

(2) In so far as teachers who have completed the secondary school course are concerned, the commission recommended the following scales of pay:

   (a) The minimum pay of a primary school teacher who has completed the secondary school course should be Rs. 100. This minimum should be given effect to immediately; and within a period of five years, it should be raised to Rs. 125.

   (b) The minimum pay of primary school teachers who have completed the secondary school course and are trained, should be Rs. 125; and within a period of five years, it should be raised to Rs. 150.

   (c) The following scales of pay should be adopted, as soon as practicable and at any rate not later than the first year of the Fifth Plan, for all primary school teachers who have completed the secondary school course and are trained:

There is one exception to this rule. As stated already, the headmasters of all higher primary schools and of lower primary schools with an enrolment of more than about 200 should be trained graduates. The salaries of trained graduates working in the above posts at the primary stage should be the same as those of trained graduates working in secondary schools. This will be discussed in the following section.

Scales of Pay of Teachers in Secondary Schools

At present, the scales of pay of teachers at the secondary stage are fixed in a rather haphazard manner and scales of remuneration do not always show a clearly integrated picture from primary school to the university. Some definite principles in fixing their pay scales and relating them to the scales of pay of primary school teachers on the one hand and those of the university teachers on the other must be followed. In this context, the commission suggested the following:

(1) The scales of pay fixed for headmasters of lower and higher secondary schools should have a definite relationship with those of the teachers in affiliated colleges or even in universities. Depending upon the quality, size and function of the school and the qualifications of the person concerned, the salary scales of the headmasters of lower secondary schools should be the same as those of junior or senior lecturers or readers. In the higher secondary schools, the principals or headmasters should be entitled to the scales of pay of a reader and, in some selected institutions, even to that of a professor. This would help to, lessen the gap between salaries at the school and university levels.

(2) On the basis of their general education, the assistant teachers in secondary schools can be divided into two categories: graduates and those with postgraduate qualifications. The relative proportions of these two categories should be definitely prescribed. The commission recommended that,

depending upon the size, function and quality of school, the proportion of teachers with postgraduate qualifications should vary from about 10 to 30 per cent. It may be pointed out that by 'postgraduate' qualifications the commission mean the same type and level of qualifications as are prescribed for junior lecturers in affiliated colleges. Teachers wit other postgraduate qualifications should be fitted in the scale of pay for graduate teachers in a suitable manner.

(3) The scales of pay of trained graduate teachers should have a minimum of Rs. 220 rising to Rs. 400 in a period of about 20 years. There should be a selection grade which would rise to Rs. 500 and be available to about 15 per cent of the cadre.

(4) Teachers with postgraduate qualifications in higher secondary schools should have the same pay scales as those of junior lecturers, i.e., Rs. 300-600, since their academic qualifications will be the same. They should be given one increment when trained.

(5) Teachers with first or second class in B.A./B.Sc. or M.A. M.Sc. should be given advance increments in the above scale. Ail. advance increment should also be given to those who are M.Eds.

(6) Professional training should be obligatory for all secondary school teachers. It should preferably be taken before first employment. Exceptions may be made in the case of teachers with postgraduate qualifications and of first and second class graduates. They may be untrained at the time of appointment but should take professional training within three years. All untrained teachers, however, shall remain on their own starting salary and be integrated into the regular scale of pay only after professional training.

RECRUITMENT OF SCHOOL TEACHERS

As at the university stage, the improvement in the salaries of school teachers must be linked with an improvement in their qualifications and methods of recruitment. The responsibility for this will be on the State Education Departments. The qualifications of teachers will have to be prescribed by the State Board of School Education and the Education Departments, would have to devise proper procedures for their recruitment. The commission's recommendations regarding the qualifications of school teachers have been given above. In the light of these and in view of local conditions, the commission trust that the State Board of School Education would prescribe the qualifications for primary and secondary teachers in all schools-government, local authority or private. With regard to methods of recruitment, the commission made the following suggestions:

(1) *Government Schools*. The existing methods of recruitment are satisfactory.

(2) *Local Authority Schools*. With regard to local authority schools, the commission recommended the constitution of district school boards which will remain in charge of all school education within a district. They will recruit the teachers required for their schools through selection committees consisting of a representative of the district school board, the District Education Officer or his representative, and a panel of two or four persons as may be prescribed by Government.

(3) With regard to private schools, the existing position leaves much to be desired and the recruitment procedures will have to be tightened on the lines recommended earlier for affiliated colleges. Every school recognized and aided by the State Education

Department should be required to have a managing committee on which there would be representatives of the Department. The Department should also prescribe the qualifications for teachers which should e similar to those in government institutions. Every post to be filled should be filled should be adequately advertised and interviews should be held by a selection committee duly constituted by the managing committee and having on it one or more experts, depending upon the importance of the post. A report on the applications received, interviews held and final selection made should be submitted to the Department for approval. As in the case of private affiliated colleges, it will be necessary to leave the authority to appoint teachers with the managing committees of the schools. But unless a teachers is appointed after the procedure prescribed above is followed and approval is obtained, no grant-in—aid should be paid on his salary, and there should be no hesitation in withholding such approval. A discriminating approach will have to be adopted and great- er freedom in these matters should be allowed to good and efficient managements while those which fail to maintain standards or leave room for malpractice should be controlled more rigorously.

PROMOTIONAL PROSPECTS

Unfortunately, promotional prospects for teachers are poor at almost all stages, and it is this aspect, rather than the scales of pay as such, that often deters talented persons from joining the profession. Steps should therefore be taken to see that good promotional prospects are provided at all stages of education, not only for improving qualifications, but for rewarding good teaching. For this, the commission make the following proposals:

(1) School Stage.

(a) Qualified and trained teachers in primary schools should be considered for promotions to higher posts as headmasters or inspectors of schools, ordinarily meant for trained graduate teachers. About ten to fifteen per cent of these posts should be reserved for such promotions.

(b) Similarly, trained graduate teachers who have done outstanding work as teachers should be eligible for promotion to ten to fifteen per cent of the posts carrying salaries of teachers with postgraduate qualifications.

(c) it should be made possible for school teachers who show the necessary aptitude and competence to be appointed as university teachers. To help in this, the UGC should give ad hoc grants to out- standing school teachers to do research into problems of 'interest to them and incidentally to qualify themselves for work at the univer- sities.

(d) Scales of pay spread over twenty years cover too long a period. It would be desirable to introduce a system under which teachers obtain advance increments for outstanding work. About 5 per cent of teachers should be able to reach the top of the scale in about ten years, and another 5 per cent in about 15 years.

(2) University Stage. The following measures may be considered:

(a) An ad hoc temporary post in the higher grade should be created for a lecturer or a reader who has done outstanding work and who cannot be given his well-earned promotion because no suitable posts are vacant. He should then be absorbed' against an appropriate permanent post as soon as it becomes available. Before such promo- tions are Made, the work of the persons concerned should be evaluated by a specially constituted expert committee and the approval of the UGC obtained. An arrangement of this type already exists in the CSIR and ICAR.

(b) In some departments where outstanding work is done,the number of posts at the professor's level should be determined on the requirements of the department and should not be arbitrarily restricted to one.

(c) If the services of an outstanding person are to be retained or obtained at the professorial level, it should be open to the university concerned, in consultation with the UGC, to offer a suitable remuneration even beyond the special scale of Rs. 1,600- 1,800. Each case should be considered on its merits and considerable elasticity should be permitted in fixing salaries.

Relating Salaries to Costs of Living

Two other points which have often been raised in the discussions with us, deserve notice. The first of these relates to the adjustment in salaries consequent upon a rise in prices. It has been suggested that, after salaries have been revised adequately in line with present price-levels, a mechanical formula should be adopted to adjust them to future movements in the cost of living, as has been done, for instance, in the case of industrial workers. While the commission realize the need to link salaries with the cost of living the commission think that this can be better done through the principle of parity. The commission have recommended that all salaries of teachers should be reviewed every five years; and the commission have also recommended the principle of parity under which the dearness allowance to be paid to all teachers should be related to that of government servants. This will ensure adequate adjustments of salaries and allowances to movements in cost of living.

Welfare Services. A large number of suggestions have been put forward with a view to providing certain welfare services to teachers such as grant of free housing, free education for children, and free or subsidized medical facilities. While suggestions of this kind may serve as transitional measures until adequate salary scales are adopted, the commission do not think that an emphasis on such marginal benefits is the right approach to an equitable solution of the problem. The best course would bc to pay the teachers adequately so that no special benefits of this type need be offered.

One important proposal, however, needs consideration. This relates to the need to organize a general programme of welfare services for all school teachers in' each State or Union Territory. The funds for this programme should be jointly raised, teachers contributing 1 1/2 per cent of their salaries and the State contributing an equal amount. The entire amount thus raised should be administered by committees consisting of representatives of teachers and Government. There should be a State level committee to decide a broad policy, and district level committees to operate the fund in accordance with the general -policies laid down. The fund could be utilized for grants for purchase of books and equipment, travel grants, scholarships for education of children, suitable assistance in case of serious sickness or disaster, and such other unforeseen calamities. When such a general welfare fund is created for each State or Union Territory, the existing teachers welfare fund set up by the Government of India may be advantageously merged with it.

Financial Implications. An obvious objection to these proposals for improvement of remuneration can be taken on financial grounds. It may be argued that, at the present and proposed levels of expansion of education, the country does not have the resources to adopt these scales of pay. The commission realized that the increase recommended by it will lead to a substantial increase in educational expenditure. But Unless the salaries are upgraded to these or even better levels and unless a feed-back process is properly initiated and maintained, it will not be possible to improve standards, and education would be unable to make a significant contribution to national development. The future of education and consequently of the nation is at stake and the price must be paid. The commission believed that it can and should find the funds needed.

A study of the salary structure in educationally advanced countries reveals some interesting points. In some countries, e.g., the USSR, teaching is among the best professions. In most of them, a wage comparable with other professions is assured. Salaries at the University level are generally high enough to attract a reasonable proportion of the best talent in the country. The gap between the salaries of university and school teachers is narrow. Even the highest salaries show a reasonable relationship to the national dividend; and the salary is related, not so much to the institution in which the teacher works, as to his qualifications. It is because of these factors that these countries call support a large expansion of education and also attract a fair proportion of talented persons to the teaching profession.

The reorganization of the salary structure for teachers on these lines is not generally feasible in a developing country where the general situation is exactly the opposite. For instance,

— the salaries of teachers are high with reference to the national dividend;

— the salaries of teachers compare unfavourably with those of other public servants which are even higher; and

— there are wide difference, between the salaries of teachers at different levels.

The basic reason for this situation is that the salaries of the superior ranks in government service are fixed very high and without any reference to the economic capacity of the people. The origin of this is often purely historical. Under the imperial regime, the salaries of the superior government servants were fixed, not in relation to the national dividend of the Indian people, but with reference to salaries prevailing in England. Consequently, salaries of the superior government servants (who were mostly Englishmen) came to be far above the economic capacity of the Indian people. Even when Indians were recruited to government services, these salaries were not reduced because it was not politically expedient to make any marked distinction between them and the expatriate officers. Hence the salaries of government servants as a class came to be fixed at a much higher level than what the country could afford. This position did not create any difficulties so long as the total volume of governmental services was limited. But it soon became the main bottleneck preventing the proper development of all social services in general and of education in particular. A solution was, therefore, attempted by the adoption of three questionable devices:

— Even in government service, the teachers were paid lower than other categories of employees who had the same (or even inferior) qualifications and responsibilities;

— The bulk of the educational enterprise was placed, not in the public or State sector, but under local bodies-and in the private sector;

— The principle of parity was rejected and teachers in local authority and private schools were paid at lower rates.

These devious methods should be given UP forthwith. If this is done and all teachers are to be paid adequately and on the basis of parity, there are only two ways in which the problem can be solved: either the salaries of all government servants Should be reduced-which cannot be done unless all incomes are regulat- ed—or the expansion of education will have to be restricted. Since the latter is neither desirable nor possible, the basic dilemma becomes clear: the State is not able to regulate all incomes and reduce the salaries of other public servants, and it does not have the money to give Justice to teachers by raising their salaries to a level comparable to that of other Government servants.

Need for Central Assistance

The need for improving the salaries of the school teachers in a big way is justified fully on its own merits and has schools teachers in a big way is justified fully on its own merits and has become urgent, partly because of the rise in the cost of living. This urgency has been heightened by the recent revision of the salaries of university teachers which has widened the existing disparities even further. The commission, therefore, recommended that the proposals made by them regarding the improvement of salaries of schools teachers should be given effect to immediately. The second point relates to Central assistance. During the first three Plans, almost every State Government revised the salaries of teachers more than once and the assistance of the Central Government was made available, n some form or other, for most of these revisions because the expenditure on these programmes was always treated as a 'plan outlay'. The salaries of teachers are very much on the low side at present and the effort needed to raise them to satisfactory levels in huge, partly because of the size of the increment and partly because of the numbers involved.

The commission afraid that the State Governments will not be able to deal with this very significant problem quickly and adequately unless Central assistance is made available on a generous basis. We, therefore, recommended that liberal Central assistance should be given to State Governments for improving the salaries of school teachers as recommended by us. Whether this assistance is given to them through the Plans or outside the Plans is not really an important issue, although the commission are of the view that the existing practice of including this expenditure within the Plan should preferably be continued.

Retirement Benefits

Of the various schemes for retire- ment benefits now in force, probably the best is that provided by the Government of India for its employees. This includes a death-cum- retirement gratuity, pension or gratuity, depending upon the length of service performed, and a family pension. State Governments are now adopting it with certain modifications for their own employees but there are various differences between the benefits given to employees of the Central Government and those given to the employees of the State Governments. Similarly, no attempt is being made to extend the scheme to teachers in local authority and private schools.

The commission see no justification for these variations and recommended that the system of retirement benefits to teachers should be based on the principles of uniformity and parity. The principle of uniformity imlies that re- tirement benefits should be uniform for all government servants- Central and State; and the principle of parity implies that retirement benefits given to teachers in government service should, also be extended to teachers working in educational institutions conducted by local authorities and private organizations. The introduction of such uniformity and parity would not involve any large increase in expenditure and would be easier to adopt than even parity in remuneration.

Retirement Benefits for School Teachers

Interim Measures

While this is the ideal towards which administrations should. move, some alternative transitional solutions to the problem may have to be adopted. With regard to school teachers, the commission make the following recommendations:

(1) *Age of Retirement.* For government teachers, the age of retirement is 58 years in some cases, 55 years (with provision for extension up to 58) in others and in one State (West Bengal), 60 years. The same rules generally apply to teachers in local authority schools. For private school teachers, the age of retirement varies, from area to area, from 55 to 58 years and even to 60 years. In Bihar it is 62 years. In Orissa, there is no age limit for retirement and a person can work as long as he is physically fit. Until provision for adequate pension is made, it is desirable to provide for a higher age limit for retirement. The commission recommended that the normal retirement age for teachers should be 60 years; and there should be provision for extension up to 65 years provided the person is physically fit and mentally alert to discharge his duties efficiently.

(2) *Retirement Benefits.* The teachers in government schools Are provided with pension, gratuity and family pension in most States. In others, provision is made for provident fund and insurance. The Union Territories generally offer the same benefits as are given to the employees of the Central Government.

With regard to teachers working in non-government schools, most of the States provide a contributory provident fund only. Recently, however, the Triple-Benefit Scheme, which provides for provident fund, pension and insurance, is becoming popular. Originally introduced in Madras, it has now been adopted in Andhra Pradesh, Assam, Bihar, Kerala, Mysore and Uttar Pradesh. In addition, Kerala offers the same retirement benefits for teachers in non-government schools as are given to teachers in government schools, provided the former opt for the conduct and discipline rules applicable to government servants and renounce the right to participate in elections. West Bengal provides only provident fund and gratuity. The Ministry of Education has drawn up a Triple-Benefit Scheme For teachers in non-government schools which is now being adopted in the Union Territories. The commission recommended that, as an interim measure, the Triple-Benefit Scheme should be adopted for all teachers in non-government schools in all States and Union Territories.

Retirement Benefits for Teachers in Higher Education

The retirement age for teachers in higher education is ordinarily 60 years, with provision for extension generally up, to 65 years, and in a few cases, even up to 70 years. Most of the universities offer a contributory provident fund only. The rate of contribution is generally 8 1/3 per cent of the basic pay. some universities permit the teacher to contribute up to 15 per cent of his pay and their own contribution is credited, depending upon the salary, at 8 to 12 per cent. Some provide for gratuity in addition to con- tributory provident fund. hi Madras, the Triple-Benefit Scheme has been extended to university and college teachers. A decision to the same effect has also been taken by the Central universities and the details of the proposal are being worked out. The commission recommended that it would be desirable to adopt the Triple-Benefit Scheme for all univer- sity and college teachers. Where a scheme of provident fund is in operation-whether for school or college teachers,-we suggest the following changes:

(1) At present, a teacher begins to contribute to the provident fund only after he becomes permanent. The contribution to the provident fund, which is a compulsory form of saving, should begin right from the first day of a teacher's career. The commission, therefore, recommended that all teachers whether temporary or permanent, should be required to contribute to the provident fund.

(2) The contribution of the employers to the provident fund of a teacher should be paid from month to month and the present rule that the teacher is not entitled to get employer's contribution if he leaves the service within five years, should be rescinded. It serves no useful purpose and is patently unfair to the teachers.

(3) At present, the amounts of the contributory provident funds of teachers are generally invested in the Postal Savings Bank where a separate account is maintained for each teacher. This has obvious administrative advantages. But financially, it is a very disadvantageous procedure. The rate of interest on deposits in Postal Savings Bank is only four per cent, though for long-term deposits like provident funds the rate of interest should be six per cent or more.

Conditions of Work

In creative work like teaching or research, the provision of stimulating conditions of work and adequate opportunities for professional advancement are extremely important and can play a very significant role in attracting and retaining the right type of persons in the profession. The conditions of work in educational institutions should be such as to enable teachers to function at their highest level of efficiency. This would imply the provision of certain minimum facilities in the classroom, essential teaching aids, library and laboratory facilities, and the maintenance of a manageable pupil-teacher ratio. it will also imply a system which encourages initiative, experimentation and creativity and gives ade- quate freedom to teachers in the organization of their courses and in the use of methods and techniques they consider most suitable. The hours, of work should be similar to those of other public servants, account being taken, not only of actual classroom teaching, but also of other work connected with it, such as study and preparation, cor- rection of exercises, evaluation, organization of co-curricular and extra-curricular activities, tutorials, seminars and other programmes of student guidance.

Adequate facilities should also be provided for professional growth through seminars, summer institutes, grants for the purchase of books or conduct of research, liberal facilities for study and sabbatical leave for self-renewal, and adequate prospects for promotion to higher cadres. The commission also recommended that a scheme should be drawn up under which every teacher should get a concessional railway pass to any part of India once in five years on payment of a reasonable contribution related to his salary.

Parity in the Terms and Conditions

The terms and conditions of service of teachers in government and local authority service are fairly satisfactory, except in one major particular: that the academic and civic freedom of these teachers is often severely restricted. The conduct and discipline rules applicable to teachers in government service (and these are generally extended to teachers in local authority service as well) are the same as for all other government employees. There is no reason why this should be so. Each profession Should have separate conditions of service; and the conduct and discipline rules for teachers should provide academic freedom which is essential to enable them to function efficiently. Moreover, existing conduct and discipline rules were mainly framed under a foreign regime when control of the political views of teachers was a major objective of official policy. Unfortunately, these rules, which have long become obsolete, are still substantially in force. It would, therefore, be desirable to frame separate and new conduct and discipline rules for teachers in government service, which would ensure them the freedom required for professional efficiency and advancement.

In so far as private schools are concerned, the difficulties are of two kinds: several private managements have not framed proper terms and conditions of service; and not infrequently, the services of teachers are terminated on inadequate grounds and without regard to fairness and justice. To meet the first of these difficulties, the commission recommended the adoption of the principle of parity and suggest that the terms and conditions of service of teachers in government and private schools should be the same. This will confer some material benefits on the teachers in private schools and give greater academic freedom to teachers in government schools. As a general practice, the services of a teacher should be terminated only after the prescribed procedure is followed and he is, given adequate opportunity to defend himself. in all cases, there should be an appeal to an arbitration tribunal consisting of a representative of the teacher, a representative of' the management and a representative of the Department.

Residential Accommodation

The problem of residential accommodation is of great importance. Difficulties often arise in the rural areas when no residential accommodation is available locally and the teacher is compelled to stay in another locality. This interferes with the efficiency of his work and prevents him from building up proper contacts with parents or undertaking programmes of adult education. These and such other problems would be eliminated if it were possible to provide reasonable residential accommodation for teachers in the locality itself.

The Kothari commission recommended that every effort should be made to increase residential accommodation for teachers in rural areas. it should be regarded as a responsibility of the local community to provide such accommodation. Wherever necessary and possible, State subsidies should be made available for the pro- gramme. In urban areas, and particularly in big cities, the problem is sometimes easier and sometimes more difficult than in villages. A programme of building construction and grant of adequate house-rent allowances in all big cities to enable teachers to obtain decent housing facilities is needed. Cooperative housing schemes for teachers should be encouraged and loans for construction of houses should be made available on favourable terms.

In the universities and affiliated colleges, it is necessary to provide residential accommodation. General experience has been that universities which provide residential accommodation to teachers have been able to obtain the services of eminent teachers and to retain them. The target to be reached over the next 20 years should be to provide residential accommodation to about 50 per cent of the teachers in the universities and to 20 per cent in affiliated colleges.

Additional Earnings

The problem of additional earnings of teachers, over and above their salaries, deserves consideration. At the school stage, the chief source of additional earnings to teachers is private tuitions. This practice prevails largely in urban areas and, in many places, complaints are made that it has become almost a scandal. The commission realize that some children (these may be gifted children preparing to excel in examinations or backward ones who may need special aid to come up to the ordinary level) will need extra assistance from the teachers. In the commission's opinion, such assistance should be provided, on an institutional basis, by the school itself The teachers concerned should be adequately remunerated and the cost should be met partly by charging special fees and partly from school funds.

At the university stage, the chief source of additional remuneration is part-time consultancy to government or industry, or remuneration from additional work, such as research carried out by the department, or fees for evaluating examination scripts. Such additional earnings should be permitted, though care should be exercised to see that the concession is not abused and that the work of the department does not suffer. The existing practice under which a teacher is required to pay a part of his earnings to the employing authority is, unfair. According to the commission such payment should not be required where the earnings do not exceed 50 per cent of the salary. If they exceed this amount, a progressive reduction may be made.

Civic Rights

The Kothari commission attach great importance to the civic freedom of teachers. It consider the participation of teachers in social and public life to be highly desirable in the interest of the profession and the educational service as a whole, and that such participation will enrich the social and political life of the country. Teachers should be free to exercise all civic rights enjoyed by citizens and should be eligible for public offices at the local, district, State or national levels. No legal. restriction should be placed on their participation in elections. When they do so, they should be expected to proceed on leave during the election campaign and to relinquish temporarily their teaching duties if the requirements of public office interfere with their proper discharge. Such participation should be in a purely personal capacity and care should be taken to see that the institution which the teacher serves or his students are not involved in it.

Women Teachers

Some discussion is needed regarding two important categories of teachers with special problems-women teachers, especially for rural areas, and teachers for tribal localities. At present, women teachers form the majority at the pre-primary stage. At other stages, the proportion of women teachers has been continually increasing in the post-Independence period as the statistics in Table 3.5 will show.

It will be seen that the number of women teachers in lower primary schools has increased from 82,000 to 200,000 or from 18 to 24 per 100 men teachers. In the higher primary schools, where the demand for women teachers is great, especially in rural areas, their number has increased from 13,000 to 140,000 or from 18 to 37 per 100 men teachers. in secondary schools and colleges of arts and science, the increase is not so large, but shows steady progress. It is only in vocational schools and colleges-and this is not unexpected-that their number is still very limited.

It is necessary to emphasize the need for the employment of women teachers in increasing proportions. At the lower primary stage, they make good teachers; and in many rural areas, the presence of a woman teacher will bring more girls to schools. At the higher primary stage, the employment of women teachers and the conduct of special schools for girls will be necessary for some years to come in most of our rural areas. In secondary schools and colleges of arts and science, the proportion of institutions for girls is continually increasing. These are mostly staffed by women teachers. Even in the remaining institutions, a large majority are really mixed institutions with some proportion of girls attending. In all of them, it should be a rule to have at least one woman teacher on the staff and where the number of girls is large, at least one woman teacher for every 30 girls. Girls are also increasingly attending vocational schools and this emphasizes the need for the employment of more women teachers in them.

This problem was examined in detail by the National Committee on Women's Education which has made a number of useful recommendations on the subject. For convenience of reference, however, the commission would highlight the following recommendations:

(1) The employment of women teachers should be encouraged at all stages and in all sectors of education.

(2) Opportunities for part-time employment of women teachers should be provided on a large scale in order to enable married women to look after their homes in addition to teaching,

(3) Residential accommodation should be provided for women teachers, particularly in rural areas, on a priority basis.

(4) In order to get women teachers to work in rural areas in adequate numbers, the scheme of condensed courses for adult women which is now being implemented by the CSWB should be expanded. Promising girls from rural areas should be given scholarships to educate and train themselves to become teachers.

(5) Many women cannot remain away from their homes for long periods as is often required in courses of professional training or of further general education. They will, however, be greatly benefited by private study and correspondence education. These facilities should be specially provided for them.

(6) Wherever necessary, special allowances may be given to women teachers working in rural areas.

Teachers for Tribal Areas

Equally important is the need to secure the services of good teachers for tribal areas. It will be necessary to give special allowances to such teachers because they have to live under very trying conditions. Assistance may also have to be provided for the education of their grown-up children. Residential accommodation is very often a must as no rented buildings are available in places where the tribals live.

It is also desirable to provide some special training to teachers who are going to work in tribal areas. This should include a study of the tribal language or languages and of tribal culture. In States where there is a large tribal population, special institutions will have to be set up to provide orientation courses to teachers posted to tribal localities. Encouragement should also be given to tribal young men and women to become teachers in the schools of these areas.

Teachers' Organizations

Teachers' organizations in all parts of the world have followed, or are following an almost identical pattern of growth: starting as 'trade unions' designed to fight for material benefits and gradually becoming bodies concerned with many aspects of their members' lives. The National Union of Teachers in the UK, for instance, was founded in 1870 because of a desperate need to improve salaries and conditions of work. Since then it has broadened its functions enormously, though it still continues to be active and increasingly successful in negotiating material benefits for its members. In India also, teachers' organizations are developing on the same broad lines.

Most of them are currently engaged, and rightly so, in securing better salaries and conditions of work for teachers. But some of them have already started other programmes of academic work and are conducting research, organizing in service education and producing literature needed by teachers. On the whole, however, the teachers organizations have still a long way to go, especially in the development of their academic programmes. While the States can assist in this undertaking, it is essentially a task for the teachers themselves. Some of the functions of teachers' organizations will be

— to secure for their members, individually and collectively, their rightful status-social, economic and professional;

- to safeguard their professional interests and to secure satisfactory conditions of work and service;
- to secure the professional growth of teachers through refresher courses, seminars, publications, library service and research;
- to work for the improvement of education in response to the challenge of the ever-changing socio-economic situation;
- to improve the teaching of subjects through the establishment of subject-teachers' associations; and
- to establish a professional code of conduct for teachers and to ensure that it is followed by members.

Professional organizations of teachers fulfilling the above functions and having a responsible and representative body of members should be recognized by the Central and State Governments. Such recognition should entitle them to the right of being consulted on all matters relating to school education, general and professional education of teachers, and their salaries and conditions of work and service.

Joint Teachers' Councils

On the lines of the scheme recently approved by the Government of India for consultative machinery and compulsory arbitration for Central Government employees, the commission recommended that the constitution of joint teachers' councils in each State and Union Territory. These councils should consist of representatives from teachers' organizations and officers of the Education Departments, with the Secretary, Education Department, as chairman. These would meet as often as necessary but at least once in six months. Their scope and functions will include all matters relating to conditions of service and work, welfare service of teachers of all categories, and general programmes for the improvement of education. The councils will be advisory bodies; but there would be a convention that, subject to the final authority of the State Cabinet, agreements reached at the council shall become operative. If there is a total failure of negotiations, compulsory arbitration should be provided for in respect of matters of pay and allowances, hours of work and leave. The joint teachers' councils will create a forum where the officers of the Department will meet the representatives of teachers' organizations at a sufficiently high level. The commission trust that this would help to build good relations between teachers and the State Governments and promote the cause of education by smoothening the innumerable administrative problems which are not promptly dealt with and which, by causing much avoidable suffering and inconvenience to teachers, have an adverse effect on educational standards.

The efficiency of the teaching profession and its contribution to national development in general and educational improvement in particular, will depend largely on its social status and morale. This will, in its turn, depend upon two interrelated factors: economic status and civic rights of teachers, and their professional competence, character and sense of dedication. Throughout the world, the general experience has been that, as the material rewards of teachers are elevated, it becomes possible to recruit into the profession individuals of a continually improving quality and with more extended professional training; and in propor- tion as the competence, integrity and dedication of teachers has increased, society has been increasingly willing and Justifiably so to give greater recognition to their material and economic status.

National Awards for School Teachers

For some years past, the Ministry of Education has been operating a scheme of national awards for school teachers.*35 The principal object of the scheme is to grant recognition to school teachers who have done outstanding work and helped to raise the status of the teaching profession. By and large, the scheme has worked fairly well. The commission requested the Ministry of Education to examine the following suggestions regarding this scheme to improve its effectiveness:

(1) The number of awards is very small at present. According to the commission, there should be about 500 awards. At the primary stage, it is very difficult to compare the merits of teachers working under entirely different conditions. We, therefore, suggest that, broadly speaking, an award should be given every year to a primary teacher from each district. For secondary teachers there should be about 200 awards in all given on a State-basis as at present.

(2) In order to minimize the influence of non-educational considerations such as politics or caste, it is desirable to strengthen the selection committees for the awards at all levels. With the committees at the State level, some outstanding non-official educationists and teachers known for their integrity and public status should be associated, and to the extent possible, this should also be done in the district-level committees.

(3) The travelling allowance given to the teachers receiving awards should be on the same basis as for Class I officers of the Government of India. The arrangements for their stay in Delhi should be comfortable and generous.

6

Recommendations for Educational Equality

One of the important social objectives of education is to equalize opportunity, enabling the backward or underprivileged classes and individuals to use education as a lever for the improvement of their condition. Every society that values social Justice and is anxious to improve the lot of the common man and cultivate all available talent, must ensure progressive equality of opportunity to all sections of the population. This is the only guarantee for the building up of an egalitarian and human society in which the exploitation of the weak will be minimized.

Inequalities of educational opportunities anise in various ways. In places where no primary, secondary, or collegiate institutions exist, children do not have the same opportunity as those who have these facilities in the neighbourhood. This handicap should be overcome by the widest dispersal of educational institutions, consistent with economy and efficiency, by instituting, an adequate scholarship programme, by providing the needed hostel facilities or by making suitable transport arrangements. It is sometimes not fully appreciated that there are at present glaring imbalances of educational development in different parts of the country: the educational developments in the States show wide differences, and even wider differences are found between the districts. To remove such inequalities, deliberate policies of equalization of educational opportunities and educational development in the different districts will have to be adopted.

Another cause of inequality of educational opportunity is the poverty of a large section of the population and the relative affluence of a small minority. Even in the neighbourhood of an educational institution, children from poor families do not have the same chance as those who come from richer ones. To overcome these handicaps, it is desirable to abolish fees progressively, to provide free books, stationery and even school meals and uniforms. In addition, it is necessary to develop a large programme of scholarships.

Again, differences in the standards of schools and colleges create an extremely intractable form of educational inequality. When admission to an institution such as a university or professional college, is made on the basis of marks obtained at the public examination at the end of the secondary stage, as often happens, the marks do not at all provide a common yardstick for a student from a rural area who attends an ill-equipped school in his village, and a student from an urban area who attends a good city school. To overcome this to some extent at least, it is necessary to evolve more reliable and egalitarian methods of selection, whether for admission to institutions or for award of scholarships.

Gross inequalities arise from differences in home environments. A child from a rural household or an urban slum having nonliterate parents, does not have the same opportunity which a child from an upper class home with highly educated parents has. These inequalities are obviously the most difficult to overcome and here progress essentially depends on the general improvement in the standard of living of the population. But something can be done by ensuring that special attention at school is paid to children from the under-privileged groups and by the provision of day-study centres or boarding houses.

Two other forms of educational 'inequalities, which are peculiar to the Indian situation, need attention. The first is the wide disparity between the education of boys and girls at all stages and in all sectors of education. The second is the equally wide, or sometimes wider disparity of educational development between the advanced classes and the backward ones-the Scheduled Castes and the Scheduled Tribes. On grounds of social justice as well as for the furtherance of democracy, it is essential to make special efforts to equalize educational opportunities between these groups.

Like all ideals in life, perfect equality of educational opportunity is probably unattainable. In such matters, however, the essence of the problem is not the attainment of the goal, but an impassioned faith and earnest striving. In a good system of education, there should be a continuous attempt to identify factors which tend to create significant forms of inequality and to adopt measures either to eliminate them altogether or at least to reduce them to the minimum.

Fees in Education

The attitude towards tuition fees has undergone several changes in our modern educational history. In 1854, the Wood's Education Despatch, which laid the foundation for the present system of education, 'insisted that some fee, however small, should be charged in all institutions on two grounds: people do not value anything which is given free; and the payment of a fee is an indication of the seriousness of purpose on the part of a student or his guardian. This view soon gave way to a concept of fees as a source of revenue for supporting schools; and in 1946-47, fees accounted for 25.6 per cent of the total educational expenditure. Since then dependence on fees as a source of revenue is diminishing and Government is assuming an increasing burden in the financing of education.

The incidence of fees varies from stage to stage and from one type of educational institution to another. The percentage of students paying fees, the rates of fees, the type of institution charging fees and the total amount of fees collected-all show considerable variations.

It will be seen that pre-primary education is mostly supported by fees. Fees have almost disappeared at the lower primary stage; but they do play a more significant role at the higher primary stage. Their contribution becomes very important at the secondary stage where the fees collected form 45.8 per cent of all fees collected in the educational system, and where they contribute 39.2 per cent of the total expenditure on secondary schools. The position in vocational schools, universities, colleges of arts and science, and colleges of professional education is broadly similar; the proportion of freestudentships is comparatively small; the fee collected per student is comparatively high; and the revenue from fees contributes a sizable amount towards the expenditure of the institutions concerned.

It is undesirable to regard fees as a source of revenue. They are the most regressive form of taxation, fall more heavily on the poorer classes of society and act as an anti-egalitarian force. Suggestions have been made to make them progressive by relating them, on a graduated scale, to the income of the parent and the size of the family. But this would not be administratively feasible and, in a country where sixty per cent of the population has an income of less than Rs. 20 per head per month, their yield would be almost negligible. It would, on the whole, be much better to raise the required revenue in some other and more equitable form than to depend on fees. The Kothari Commission recommend, therefore, that the country should gradually work towards a stage when all education would be tuition-free. The implementation of this programme, however, would have to be spread over a period of time and the abolition of tuition fees will have to proceed from stage to stage, beginning with primary. It may be mentioned that school education is completely free in most countries, and all education from elementary school to the research degree is free in the USSR.

Fees at the Primary Stage

The Constitution requires the provision of free and compulsory education for all children up to the age of 14 years. Even though the 'compulsory' part of this directive may take about 20 years to realize, the 'free' part of it should be implemented without delay. We, therefore, recommend that all tuition fees at the primary stage should be abolished as early as possible and preferably before the end of the Fourth Five Year Plan. This implies that there would be no tuition fees in government, local authority and aided private schools, grants-in-aid to the last group being suitably adjusted. Fee-charging independent private schools which receive no aid may, however, continue to exist.

Fees at the Secondary Stage

At the secondary stage, the problem is a little more difficult. Two arguments have been put forward in favour of the levy of fees at this stage. The first is that the expansion of secondary education being still largely restricted to the middle and upper classes of the society, the abolition of fees will be more in favour of the haves than of the have-nots, and the second is that the revenue from fees collected at this stage being substantial, the abolition of fees would be neither feasible nor desirable from the financial point of view. The Kothari Commission didn't agree with either of these arguments.

The levy of fees in secondary schools prevents several children from the poorer classes of society, and particularly girls, from receiving education and it is mostly among these groups that the expansion of secondary education will have to take place in the next two decades. The abolition of fees at the secondary stage is thus intended mainly for the benefit of such underprivileged groups who are now entering secondary education in large numbers. It is also necessary to point out that the total revenue from fees collected at the secondary stage has declined considerably in the Third Five Year Plan. Madras has made all education free till the end of the secondary stage. Uttar Pradesh and Orissa have made it free for girls. Mysore, which had already introduced a very large programme of free-studentships, has now decided to follow Madras from the current year. The Kothari Commission understood that Andhra Pradesh is also proposing to adopt the same policy. Maharashtra and Gujarat now provide free-studentships to nearly 85 per cent of the total enrolment. In Punjab, Madhya Pradesh and Rajasthan, it is free for girls in all government schools at least and very largely free for boys also. In all parts of the country, it has always been free for the Scheduled Castes, the Scheduled Tribes and some other backward classes. If all these developments are duly allowed for, it appears that the provision of tuition-free secondary education is limited only in Assam, Bihar, Orissa (for boys), Uttar Pradesh (for boys) and West Bengal. The difficulty of making secondary education free of tuition or of finding alternative sources for the loss of revenue involved is thus no longer as formidable as it was five years ago.

There was a view in the Commission that the levy of tuition fees must continue to be the rule for lower secondary education, tempered by adequate and suitable provision for the grant of concessions and exemptions to all the needy students. On a careful consideration of the problem, however, such a system does not have much to commend itself and involves several administrative difficulties. The Commission, therefore, recommend that lower secondary education should be made tuition-free in all government, local authority and aided private institutions as early as possible and, preferably before the end of the Fifth Plan. Even where It is not possible to implement this recommendation in one step, a beginning should be made by making all vocational secondary education free; and as resources permit, the principle should be extended to girls and to children who come from the poorer families.

Fees in Higher Education

At present, fees play an important role in higher education. In 1960-61 fees contributed 37.4 per cent of the total expenditure on universities, 48.5 per cent of that on colleges of general education, 22.2 per cent of that in colleges of professional education (excluding teacher training), 15.9 per cent in colleges for special education and 12.8 per cent in colleges of teacher training. For higher education as a whole, the contribution of fees was as high as 37.3 per cent of the total expenditure. This is even larger than that in the educationally advanced and richer countries. In the United States, for instance, only about 25 per cent of the income of institutions of higher learning is derived from fees and in Britain, it is less than oneeighth.

The Kothari Commission did not advocate the immediate general abolition of fees in higher education, although this should be the ultimate goal of educational policy. This programme has a lower priority than that of making all school education free and should be considered only after tuition fees have been abolished in secondary schools. At present, when higher education is mostly being availed of by the top five per cent of the population, a policy of levying fees combined with that of liberal provision of free-studentships to all the needy and deserving students would prove to be better than that of general abolition of fees. We, therefore, recommend that, for the next ten years, the main effort with regard to fees in higher secondary and university education should be to expand the provision of tuition-free education to cover all the needy and deserving students. To begin with, the proportion of free-studentships should be increased to at least 30 per cent of the total enrolment. The Commission also commend, for general acceptance, policies which have been adopted in some areas to provide tuition-free higher education to underprivileged groups, e.g., provision of free-studentships to Scheduled Castes, Scheduled Tribes, girls, or children of persons whose income is below a prescribed level. This will be adequate to meet the social demand from the underprivileged sections of society that are now in secondary schools and are quickly moving up to seek admission to institutions of higher education. The problem may be reviewed again after ten years.

Other Private Costs

The private costs of education required for textbooks, supplies, co-curricular activities, etc., have increased very substantially in recent years and amount not infrequently, to several times the tuition fees. in fact, the greater financial burden that creates the non-egalitarian trends todav is not so much tuition-fees

At present, the proportion of free-studentships to total enrolment in institutions of higher education is very small 14.6 per cent of students get tuition-free education in universities, 15.1 per cent in colleges of general education, 12.1 per cent in colleges of professional education, and 47.6 per cent in colleges of special education (1960-61 figures). as these other costs. The Commission carried out a small study to discover the approximate level of these indirect costs at the school stage. For this purpose, the Commission selected a few schools with varying levels of such costs in each State and Union Territory and collected detailed information from them.

Parents are required to incur very heavy expenditure for this purpose. Consequently, only a small proportion of children have all the books at the beginning of the school year; a much larger proportion have them, not at the beginning of the school year, but towards the middle or even the end. Not infrequently, a proportion of students have no books at all. This has a very adverse effect on standards. We, therefore, recommend that an earnest effort be made to reduce these private costs of education. They are often raised thoughtlessly or for snobbish rather than for educational reasons. Side by side a programme should immediately be developed for providing at least textbooks, if not stationery also, free of charge (or at concessional rates) to all students (or at least to all the needy and deserving students). This would be a crucial programme for the qualitative improvement of education. Obviously, the manner of its implementation will have to vary from one stage of education to another.

(1) *Primary Stage*. At the primary stage, a programme of providing free textbooks should be given very high priority and introduced immediately. It should also be extended to the higher primary stage as early as possible. Children freshly joining schools should be

welcomed at a school function and presented with a set of books. Others should be presented with a complete set of books for the succeeding year as soon as the results of the annual examinations are declared and before the long vacation starts, so that they can make some use of the vacations for further study.

(2) *Secondary and University Stages.* A programme of book-banks should be developed in secondary schools and in institutions of higher education. In addition, the libraries of these institutions should contain a large number of sets of textbooks so that every student can have access to them in the library or the reading-room. The State Education Departments should have a fund at their disposal from which they could encourage the establishment of book-banks in secondary schools; and a similar fund should be placed at the disposal of the UGC which could organize them in the universities and affiliated colleges. The programme should be developed on so large a scale that every needy student in a secondary school or institution of higher education will be provided with a set of all the textbooks needed at the beginning of the school year or have easy access to them in the library.

(3) *Grants for Purchase of Books.* Grants for the purchase of books should be made to the more talented of the students. The Kothari Commission recommend that the top 10 per cent of the students in educational institutions (subject to a means test, if necessary) should be given small grants annually for the purchase of books, which need not necessarily be textbooks. The scheme should be begun in the universities and later extended to affiliated colleges and secondary schools.

Scholarships

The programme of scholarships has received considerable emphasis in recent years. The total expenditure on scholarships has increased from Rs. 34.5 million or 3 per cent of the total educational expenditure in 1950-51 to about Rs. 420 million or 7 per cent of the total educational expenditure in 1965-66. A careful study of the position, however, shows that an attempt will have to be made to reorient and expand the existing scholarship programmes on the following lines:

The scholarship programme is a continuous process and has to be organized at all stages of education. At present there is a fairly well-organized programme in higher education and vocational courses, although even here, much expansion is needed. But as there is no adequate programme at the school stage, a good deal of talent is already eliminated by the time the threshold of university entrance is reached. The provision of scholarships in higher education does not, therefore, prove as helpful as it might otherwise have been.

It has not been possible to evolve a good method of selecting awarders for scholarships. At present, most scholarships are awarded on the basis of marks obtained in some public examination; and as these tend to favour students from the well-to-do homes or good urban schools, scholarships do not really help potentially talented students whose preparation has remained inadequate for no fault of theirs. A more equitable and egalitarian basis for the award of scholarships has, therefore, to be evolved.

If the best results are to be obtained, a scholarship programme should be accompanied by a placement programme whose objective is to ensure that the scholarship holders are placed in good institutions and a further complementary programme of ensuring that an adequate number of institutions which maintain fairly high standards is available at all stages.

A careful watch will have to be kept at all points of transfer from one stage or sub-stage of education to another to ensure that all the abler students (at least the top 5-15 per cent of the enrolment, depending upon the stage of education) do continue their studies further.

An adequate machinery to administer the programme would have to be created and the operation of the programme fully decentralized to avoid the procedural delays and other difficulties that are experienced at present.

In the light of these broad principles the Commission indicated below the manner in which scholarship programmes should be reorganized at the different stages of education.

Scholarships at the Primary Stage

Steps should be taken to ensure that, at the end of the lower primary stage (class IV or V), no 'Promising' child is Prevented from continuing his studies further on account of non-availability of a school, or of socioeconomic difficulties; and to this end, scholarship of an adequate amount will have to be provided to every child that may need it. In addition, it will be desirable to evolve a placement programme and to try to place the brighter children to the extent possible in the good schools that may be available at this stage. The Kothari Commission have assumed that the target should be to provide scholarships for 2.5 per cent of the enrolment at the higher primary stage by 1975-76 and to 5 per cent of the same enrolment by 1985-86.

Scholarships at the Secondary Stage

The main object of the scholarship programmes to be

developed at the secondary stage would be to ensure that, under any circumstances, the top 15 per cent of the children in the age-group do get transferred to secondary schools and that their further education is not prevented by poverty. In this context, the Commission made the following concrete suggestions:

(1) The present system of awarding scholarships on a centralized basis such as a district or a block, tends to be unfair to students who have attended the weaker schools and who, in consequence, show an inferior level of preparation for no fault of theirs. While this system should be continued and even expanded, the Commission recommend that as a supplement to it, about 10 per cent of students in class VII or VIII in each school should be assisted, to the extent necessary, to continue their studies further. Taking the system as a whole, the target should be to provide scholarships to 5 per cent of the enrolment by 1975-76 and to 10 per cent of the enrolment by 1985-86.

(2) The existing programme of scholarships would have to be considerably expanded to meet the demands of the situation. Wherever necessary, hostel facilities will also have to be provided.

(3) To begin with, one good secondary school (with adequate residential facilities) should be developed in each community development block and about 10 per cent of urban schools should also be similarly covered. Access to these schools should be mainly on the basis of talent; and an adequate placement programme should be developed at this stage-this does not exist at all at present-to help the gifted students and the scholarship-holders to get admission to these schools.

The responsibility for the development of this comprehensive programme should be squarely placed on the Education Departments which should work in collaboration with the universities. The secondary stage is the most crucial for discovery and development of talent, and unfortunately, it is precisely at this stage that the scholarship programme is now weak. Its development will, therefore, have to be accorded high priority.

The Kothari Commission were aware of the great difficulties and lack of reliable criteria and techniques for identifying talent. We, therefore, recommend that steps should be taken immediately to devise suitable techniques for identifying talent at this stage. Each State should organize a testing service at the end of the primary stage (class VII or VIII) and also at the end of the lower secondary stage (class X) and make its assistance available to all the schools. The details of the organization of this service, under a new body called the State Evaluation Organization, has been discussed elsewhere. If properly developed, this service could be of considerable help to students and institutions; they would obtain some useful information about their performance in relation to the district, State or even the national average level of attainment; and such information, apart from its utility to students and parents, would also be of great assistance to the Education Departments in the award of scholarships.

Two further points need mention. The first is that every educational institution should be assisted to develop a programme for identifying the brighter children attending it and for providing them with special enrichment programmes to suit their needs and to help in their growth. These programmes, the nature of which would very from stage to stage and from one type of institution to another, would have to be carefully designed and teachers would have to be trained in putting them across. Secondly, in all these programmes, 'talent' should not be understood in the traditional sense only, but should cover a, wide range of mathematical, verbal, artistic and experimental skills. Scholarships and encouragement should be available, on a basis of equality, to all talent at all stages of education.

Scholarships at the University Stage

The programme of scholarships in higher education is extremely important. The bulk of the existing programme is in this sector and a very large part of it is provided by the Government of India. In the Commission's opinion, a further development on the following lines is needed: increase in the number of scholarships and other forms of student aid and in the amount of scholarships; reduction of procedural and other delays; improving the methods of selecting awardees; institution of scholarships for study abroad; and institution of a large programme of loan scholarships. The Commission's recommendations on these and other allied matters are given below.

Number of Scholarships

According to the Commission, the ultimate target towards which we should move in the provision of scholarships at the university stage would be the following:

(1) Scholarships should be available to at least 15 per cent of the enrolment at the undergraduate stage by 1976 and to 25 per cent of such enrolment by 1986; and

(2) Scholarships should be available to at least 25 per cent of the enrolment at the postgraduate stage by 1976 and to 50 per cent of such enrolment by 1986.

These targets should be treated as national averages and it should be an objective policy to vary them from institution to institution or from faculty to faculty. For example, a much larger proportion of scholarships should be available in university departments and colleges. The proportion of scholarships available in affiliated colleges should generally be lower; but in good colleges, it may be higher than and even equal to, that in the universities. Similarly, the proportion of scholarships in courses in science could be greater than that in legal education. Even more liberal scholarships could be given to teachers under training.

Amount of Scholarships

At present, the amount of scholarships at a given level is the same for all students. For instance, the post-matriculation scholarship is of Rs. 50 p.m. in the first year and its amount remains the same for a student who stays with his parents and attends the college in Ms town or city as well as for another who has to leave his family and stay in a hostel to join a college or a university. Similarly, the amount of the Central scholarship is generally uniform for all parts of the country, irrespective of the fact that a place like Delhi is far costlier than a mofussil town. No studies are also conducted to find out the expenditure which a student has to incur in hostels or on items like purchase of books, equipment, etc. Hardly any serious attempt is made to keep costs down. The Kothari Commission have carefully examined the problem and make the following recommendations:

(1) Two kinds of scholarships would ordinarily be needed for those who have to stay in hostels: these should cover all the direct and indirect costs of education (i.e., tuition fees, books, supplies, etc.) and living costs; and for those who can stay at home: these should mainly cover direct and indirect costs.

(2) Studies should be continuously carried out to ascertain the direct and indirect costs, as well as the hostel charges, which students have to bear. This

should be one of the studies which each university should undertake and periodically repeat. A continuous attempt should be made to keep the direct and indirect costs to the minimum. Everywhere, hostel costs are rising and very often, the increase is not justified. An attempt has to be made to keep the hostel costs down to the minimum. The number of 'servants' in hostels should be reduced and gradually eliminated altogether. It is a part of education that students should learn to look after themselves and not be dependent on servants to serve meals, make beds, etc. Selfservice should be the rule rather than the exception. This will make it possible to keep the value of scholarships down and to extend the benefit of financial assistance to a larger number of students.

National Scholarships

The national scholarships form another important category of scholarships awarded at the university stage. The entire expenditure on these scholarships which were instituted in the Third Five Year Plan and are awarded on the basis of merit, is met by the Government of India. In actual practice, the Government of India allocates a specified number of scholarships to each State Government and the award is made, under the rules framed by the Government of India, by the State Government concerned. This is a good scheme and should be continued and largely expanded. The Kothari Commission make the following recommendations in this regard:

(1) *Coverage*. At present, the scheme covers less than one per cent of the students who appear at the various exam examinations to which the scholarships are allocated. The target to be reached should be to cover five per cent of such students by 1975-76 and ten per cent of such students by 1985-86.

(2) *Decentralization.* In the practice now in force, the Ministry of Education allocates the scholarships to the different States on the basis of population. The allocation is further subdivided according to the different examinations held in the State and care is taken to see that at least one award is allocated to each examination irrespective of the number of students appearing therein. The names of the students eligible for these awards are communicated by the Director of Education of the State, in due course, to the Ministry of Education which then issues 'entitlement' cards to the students concerned. On the production of these cards, the students do not find any difficulty about payment of fees etc., before the scholarships are actually paid to them. This is a much simpler procedure than that which was in vogue some time ago; but even now there are delays and complaints about payments, and the procedure needs still further simplification.

One concrete suggestion in this regard is that the power to issue entitlement cards should be delegated to the authorities holding examinations to which the national scholarships have been assigned. As at present, the Ministry should allocate national scholarships to the different examinations in a State. The authorities holding these examinations should be instructed to announce the names of the winners of the national scholarships (subject to verification on the basis of the means test in due course) along with the examination results. They should also be supplied with the requisite number of entitlement cards duly signed by an officer of the Ministry of Education and these should become valid as soon as they are countersigned on behalf of the authority holding the examinations. It should also be made a rule that the entitlement card should be given to a student along with his examination result.

The institutions which the holders of national scholarships join should be under an obligation to pay them the amount of the scholarships direct, after verifying the means test. The payment should be made from mouth to month along with salaries of staff, and the institutions should claim reimbursement from the State Government in due course. This should not be difficult if the entitlement card has a perforated portion on the production of which the State Directors of Education are required to pay a year's scholarship in advance to the school authorities.

At present the Government of India makes the payment of the scholarship amount to the institutions concerned through the State Governments or the State Departments of Education. The Kothari Commission believed that a procedure on the above lines would overcome several of the difficulties at present experienced by the students.

(3) *A New Basis of Award.* For the national scholarships to be given to university entrants, the most common practice adopted at present is to award them on the basis of marks obtained in the external public examination at the end of the secondary course; and for this purpose, the entire State is regarded as a unit. As was pointed out earlier, this method is unfair to the brighter students who happen to have attended weaker schools and whose preparation, therefore, leaves much to be desired. What is needed, therefore, is the adoption of a more egalitarian basis for the award of scholarships in such cases.

From this point of view, the Commission suggest that it would be desirable to group schools in small clusters', on the basis of their enrolments and socio-economic backgrounds, and to select the top 'few' students in each duster for the award of scholarships, the actual number of students to be selected depending upon the funds available. The 'top' students in one group may not come up to the top students in other groups. But they represent good potential talent and would make good if special arrangements were made in the universities or colleges to which they are admitted, to give them some special attention and help them to make up for the shortcomings in their attainments. The general policy should be to award fifty per cent of the scholarships on the basis of school dusters and the remaining fifty per cent, as at present, on the basis of the State as a unit.

The Kothari Commission strongly recommended this new method of awarding scholarships, especially at a time when the provision of higher education will be made only on a selective basis. This egalitarian approach will secure social justice and net a much greater amount of talent than is done at present. With the expention of secondary education to rural areas, the establishment of a large number of new secondary schools every year, and the entry of young persons from the unprivileged sections of the society into secondary and higher education , students will now begin to arrive at the threshold of higher education with widely varying levels of preparation which reflect,not much the variation in native capacity, as in their socioeconomic backgrounds and in the standards of the secondary schools which they attended. Unless due allowance is made for them, the stratification of Indian society will tend to increase rather than decrease.

University Scholarships. At present, the number of scholarships awarded by the universities is extremely small both at the undergraduate and at the postgraduate stages. This is not a happy position. The Kothari Commission recommend that a scheme of university scholarships should be developed in the Fourth Plan itself and the funds required for it should be placed at the disposal of the UGC which should make them available to the universities (and which in their turn should make them available to colleges). The award of the scholarships should be made in accordance with the rules framed by the universities with the approval of the UGC; and the authority to select students for the award in accordance with the rules should be delegated to the heads of the institutions.

The target to be reached should be to cover about 10 per cent of the enrolment at the undergraduate stage and 20 per cent of such enrolment at the postgraduate stage by 1976.

These scholarships should be in the Central sector and the grants-inaid on account of them should be borne by the Government of India, through the UGC, on a permanent basis.

There is a large Central scheme of post-matriculation scholarships for the Scheduled Castes and Scheduled Tribes. This will be discussed in a later section.

At the postgraduate stage, it is necessary to secure better coordination between the different agencies which award scholarships, e.g., the University Grants Commission, the Indian Council for Agricultural Research, the Atomic Energy Commission, etc. This multiplicity is welcome because it augments the resources available for scholarships. But it often leads to anomalies in the conditions for the award of scholarship (e.g., in matters like the amount of scholarships, qualifications needed, etc.). According to the Commission think that the necessary coordination would be secured if a Standing Committee on Postgraduate and Research Scholarships is set up at the national level in the Ministry of Education consisting of the representatives of the Ministries concerned and other organizations that award scholarships in the universities for postgraduate and research work and a representative of the EaterUniversity Board. The Committee could meet about twice a year, review the programmes in operation and see that they are properly coordinated.

Scholarships in Vocational Education. At present there is much larger provision of scholarships in vocational schools and professional colleges than in schools and colleges of general education. But further improvements are needed on two lines: (a) a more egalitarian policy in admissions; and (b) a still further increase in the number of scholarships as well as in their amount.

Admissions. The Commission carried out a study of the socioeconomic backgrounds of the students who generally go to vocational schools and their implications for policies relating to admissions and scholarships. At present, most of these institutions make their own admissions and award scholarships according to rules framed for the purpose. The pressure for admissions to institution like the engineering and medical colleges has, however, led to the creation of centralized agencies for selection and placement of students. The Indian Institutes of Technology, which draw their students practically from all parts of the country, hold a common competitive examination for admission on a national basis. But as examination marks figure largely as a basis of selection, in most cases, the students admitted to the more important of these institutions generally tend to come from urban areas from good schools or from well-to-do homes.

With regard to the scholarships programme in vocational education, therefore, the Kothari Commission make the following recommendations:

(1) It is necessary to make more intensive efforts in future to introduce an egalitarian element in admissions to institutions of vocational. education and particularly to institutions like the institutes of technology and colleges of engineering and medicine.

(2) The admission examinations to the institutes of technology are held in English. This gives an undue weightage to students from English medium schools to which the rich send their children. The Kothari Commission recommend that these admission examinations should be held in English and also in the regional languages and the best students from each linguistic group should be selected, if necessary, on the basis of a quota related to population. Some of the students so selected may not be quite up to the standard in English. But this deficiency should be overcome by giving an intensive training in English to the selected students in their first year at the institutes.

(3) The proportion of scholarships in institutions of vocational education should be much larger than in those of general education. At the school stage, about 30 per cent of the students should be covered by scholarships of one type or another; and at the collegiate stage, this proportion should be raised to 50 Per cent.

Scholarships for Study Abroad

A national programme for award of scholarships to enable some of our best talented persons to go abroad for further education or training in research is also needed. Young persons so trained would be of very great use for the development of agriculture, industry, universities and research centres. We, therefore, recommend that a national programme of about 500 awards a year should be set up for this purpose.

Loan Scholarships. An important issue raised in the evidence before us relates to the general use of loan scholarships. One view was that all scholarships in higher education should be given in the form of loans only. Three arguments were put forward in support of the proposal:

— it would set up a revolving fund in 5-10 years that would greatly reduce the burden on the State revenue;

— it would prevent wasteful expenditure as students would draw only the minimum amount required for their maintenance; and

— it would help to build up character and create a sense of responsibility and self-respect in the rising generation.

The counter-argument was that a programme of loan scholarships involves innumerable administrative problems about recoveries and causes hardship to young persons who would have to begin life with a heavy load of debt. To meet this, an elaborate proposal for the establishment of a National Scholarships Foundation to be-set up by the Government of India under an Act of Parliament was advocated. This proposal visualizes that the Corporation would start functioning with a fairly big capital fund, say of Rs. 500 million or more. The interest to be charged on scholarships would be kept to the minimum, to cover only bad debts and administrative expenditure. The necessary loans would be advanced to young persons on their personal security only. Recovery would begin one year after the person begins to earn; and there would be no recovery if the earnings fall below a prescribed level. The instalments to be paid would be related to the total earnings of the Person in a graduated manner. There would also be a suitable provision for bonuses or discounts for prompt payments; and to facilitate recovery, every employer would be under an obligation to deduct the loan-repayment instalments from the salary at source, on the analogy of the Income-Tax Act.

According to the Commission, an exclusive programme of loan scholarships is non-egalitarian since it creates a disadvantage only for the economically handicapped students. It will also not be workable-unless a fair element of subsidy is provided-for students of humanities whose chances of employment and level of earning leave much to be desired. The Commission, therefore, prefer a proposal in which a programme of outright scholarships is combined with one of loan scholarships. The programme of loan scholarships in higher education should be organized on the following lines:

(1) The programme would be a supplement to that of outright scholarships which should be provided on the scale the Commission have suggested.

(2) It would be essentially meant for students in the sciences and the professional courses where the chances of employment and levels of earnings are comparatively better and are more likely to make the scheme successful. There should be no upper limit to the number of such loan scholarships in this sector and an attempt should be made to provide financial assistance to every needy student. To a limited extent and in deserving cases, the programme should be extended to cover arts students also.

(3) If a person who holds a loan scholarship joins the teaching profession, one-tenth of the loan should be written off for each year of service. This will encourage good students to join this profession.

(4) For convenient administration of the loan scholarships programme, a National Loan Scholarships Board may be set up as outlined above.

The programme of scholarships and placement at the university stage will have to be accompanied by a complementary programme of developing quality institutions. This need will be met by the development of major universities,centers of advanced study,and of at least one good college in each district.The details of these programmes are discussed elsewhere.

General Problems Relating to Student Aid

We shall now briefly discuss a few other related issues. These relate to all stages of education.

(1) *Transport.* The provision of transport facilities can help to reduce the cost on hostels and scholarships the Commission have seen schools in rural areas which provide bicycles to the students who have to come from a distance. An arrangement of this type should be encouraged, as it makes the secondary school accessible to students in outlying villages. Wherever possible, the same arrangement could also be extended to other categories of institutions.

(2) *Day-Study centres and Lodging Houses.* For students who do not have adequate facilities for study at home, it is necessary to provide a large number of day-study centres at the secondary and university stages. It would also be desirable to provide lodging houses, i.e., places where they can stay throughout the day, and even at night, but go home for food. Some institutions have tried to provide this facility by adopting an unorthodox approach i.e., by using classrooms for residential and study purposes before and after school hours and at night. Experiments of this type should be encouraged.

(3) *Earn and Learn.* Facilities for Students to earn and pay a part of their expenses should be developed on as large a scale as possible as a supplement to the programme of scholarships.

(4) *Scholarships for Girls.* In scholarships and other forms of student aid, preferential consideration should be given to the needs of girls.

Financial Responsibility about Scholarships.

About 92 per cent of the expenditure on scholarships comes from Central and State Government funds. The Central funds account for nearly one-fourth of the total expenditure. More than seventy per cent of the Central expenditure on scholarships is incurred on higher education only. The Commission's recommendations in this regard are as follows:

(1) The responsibility for developing an adequate scholarship programme at the school stage should rest with the State Governments. In higher education, it should be regarded as a responsibility of the Government of India to make adequate provision for scholarships in all institutions of higher education-general and vocational-and also for scholarships for study abroad.

(2) To develop a good programme of scholarships at the school stage, the funds needed for it should be provided in the Centrally sponsored sector in the Fourth Plan and the same basis may be continued in the Fifth Plan. The State Governments would then be able to carry it on their own.

Educational Opportunity of Handicapped Children

The education of handicapped children has to be organized not merely on humanitarian grounds, but also on grounds of utility. Proper education generally enables a handicapped child to overcome largely his (or her) handicap, and makes him a useful citizen. Social justice also demands it; it has to be remembered that the Constitutional Directive on compulsory education includes handicapped children as well. Very little has been done in this field so far; and on account of several difficulties, any great improvement in the situation does not seem to be practicable in the near future. All the same, it is important that a serious beginning is made immediately. The Commission's proposals attempt to indicate a feasible programme of action which may well lay the foundation for a more massive attack on the problem to be made in later years.

Scope and Size of the Programme. The primary task of education for a handicapped child is to prepare him for adjustment to a socio-cultural environment designed to meet the needs of the normal. It is essential, therefore, that the education of handicapped children should be an inseparable part of the general educational system. The differences lie in the methods employed to teach the child and the means the child uses to acquire information. These differences in methodology do not influence the content or the goals of education. This form of education is, therefore, conveniently referred to as 'special education'.

Determination of the size of the handicapped population has eluded educators, planners and social workers not only in this country but also in many of the economically advanced countries. For instance, even the United States does not have a reliable estimate of the number of handicapped children. From the available evidence, it appears, however, that the total population in the following categories is about 2.5 million in our country.

(1) *The Blind.* A recent survey undertaken under the auspices of the Ministry of Health has, however, suggested that the number of blind persons might be of the order of four million. This is also the estimate of the Royal Commonwealth Society for the Blind, London. The number of children of school age is estimated at 400,000.

(2) *The Deaf.* No national survey of the incidence of deafness has been undertaken. Estimates based on a few sample surveys would seem to indicate that the number of deaf persons in the country maybe anywhere between 1 million and 1.5 Million. The number of children of school-going age is believed to be about 300,000.

(3) *The Orthopaedically Handicapped.* No national survey of this category of handicapped persons has yet been undertaken. Again,based on a few sample surveys,it would appear that the number of orthopaedically handicapped children in the country is about the same as that of the blind.

(4) *The Mentally Retarded.* Mental retardation is a complex concept influenced to a large extent by cultural factors and its determination involves the administration of sophisticated psychological tests. It is, therefore, difficult to estimate the number of such children in the country. Here again, estimates based on somewhat inadequate sample surveys seem to suggest that the country may have between 1.4 million and 1.8 million mentally retarded children.

Existing Educational Facilities. The present position of educational facilities for these children is as follows:

(1) *The Blind.* At present, there are about 115 schools and other establishments for the blind with an enrolment of 5,000 or a little over 1 per cent of the total number of blind children in the country. Most of these

institutions impart primary education coupled with training in a few simple handicrafts. Music forms an integral part of the curriculum. The great majority of the existing institutions are run by voluntary agencies but are assisted by State Governments. The Central Government has set up a comprehensive National Centre for the Blind at Dehra Dun. This Centre includes a Central Braille Press which publishes textbooks and other reading material in Braille. The Centre also has a workshop for the manufacture of Braille appliances, which produces the basic equipment needed for the education of the blind. There are three centres for the training of teachers of the blind sponsored by the Government of India and they can train between 30 and 40 teachers annually. In addition, the Governments of Madras and Andhra Pradesh conduct courses for training teachers when needed.

(2) *The Deaf.* The number of schools for deaf children is about 70. Most of these schools provide primary education coupled with some pre-vocational training in engineering and non-engineering occupations. The majority are privately managed but are aided by the State Governments. The total enrolment is about 4,000 or a little over one per cent of the total population of such children. About half a dozen centres for the training of teachers of the deaf are functioning at present and can train 50 to 60 teachers per annum.

(3) *The Orthopaedically Handicapped.* The major problem of this category of children is locomotor in character and they often attend ordinary schools. At present, there are about 25 institutions for such children with a total enrolment not exceeding about 1,000. Since most orthopaedically handicapped children do not present special educational problems, it is not

considered necessary to have specially trained teachers for this category of children.

(4) *The Mentally Retarded.* On account of its complexity, this aspect of special education has received very little attention. There are only about 27 schools for mentally retarded children with a total enrolment not exceeding 2,000. One of these schools is run by the Government of India. Two centres for the training of teachers of mentally retarded children are functioning at present and they can train about 20 teachers annually.

At present, there are practically no facilities for the education of other categories of handicapped children. Some of the emotionally disturbed children are cared for in children's homes and other institutions set up under the various Children's Acts. As a rule, however, such homes are not intended primarily for the educational treatment of emotionally disturbed children.

It is evident from the brief review given in the preceding paragraphs that the existing facilities are extremely inadequate. In certain cases, the foundation has been laid while in others we have to begin at the beginning. The importance of a carefully thought-out plan for the development of educational services for the handicapped cannot, therefore, be over-emphasized.

A Plan for Action

The progress in providing educational facilities to handicapped children will be limited by two main considerations; teachers and financial resources. A reasonable target will. therefore, be to provide, by 1986, education for about 15 per cent of the blind, deaf and orthopaedically handicapped children and to about 5 per cent of the mentally retarded ones-this will mean the provision of educational facilities for about 10 per cent of the total number of handicapped children. As a part of the programme, it should be possible to have at least one good institution for the education of handicapped children in each district.

This goal can be reached through the adoption of two programmes-the special and the integrated. In the special programmes which alone have been developed so far in our country, the handicapped children are isolated from the normal ones and placed in special institutions. In the educationally advanced countries, however, a great deal of stress is now being laid on the integration of handicapped children into the regular school programmes. This has several advantages of which two are important; reduction of costs and promoting mutual understanding between handicapped and the non-handicapped children. This has also its disadvantages. For instance, many handicapped children find it psychologically disturbing to be placed in an ordinary school. On an overall view of the problem, however, we feel that experimentation with the integrated programmes is urgently required and every attempt should be made to bring in as many children into integrated programmes as possible.

In addition, it will be desirable to develop services on a pilot basis for some additional categories of children who have peculiar educational needs, viz., the partially-sightcd, the speechhandicapped, the aphasic, the brain-injured and the emotionally disturbed. As pointed out earlier, hardly any attempts have been made in this field-so far. It is impossible to state at this stage what the number of such children will be. Even the facilities for training teachers are very inadequate. The Ministry of Health is already in the process of setting up an institute for the training of speechtherapists at Bangalore. These speech-therapists could deal with speech-handicapped and aphasic children. There are hardly any facilities for the training of teachers for the partially-sighted or the emotionally disturbed and brain-injured children. We, therefore, suggest that an attempt should be made in the next two Plans, to set up a few centres as a pilot project to assist these categories of children. The whole problem may be reviewed again after 10 years.

To develop these programmes adequately, attention will have to be paid to the following matters:

(1) The preparation of teachers will need emphasis and attention. Assuming a pupil-teacher ratio of 10:1, about 16,500 teachers will be needed for the blind, deaf and mentally retarded children only. This will necessitate a considerable increase in the capacity of the existing training institutions and the establishment of new ones.

(2) It is necessary to coordinate the efforts of different agencies working in the field such as the Ministry of Education, the Central Social Welfare Board, voluntary organizations interested in the problem and the Ministry of Health. Similar coordination will also be needed at the State levels.

(3) It is also necessary to develop adequate research in the problem. The Kothari Commission recommend that the Ministry of Education should develop a programme for this and allocate the necessary funds. The NCERT should have a cell for the study of handicapped children. The principal function of this cell would be to keep in touch with the research that is being done in the country and outside and to prepare materials for the use of teachers.

Regional Imbalance

The development of educational facilities in the different parts of the country has been very uneven and one of the important objectives of educational policy should be to strive to reduce the existing imbalances to the minimum. With a view to highlighting the problem, the Commission made a special study of some of the regional imbalances as they exist between the different States and districts for the year 1960-61, the latest year for which the data are available.

It will be seen that the State income per head is lowest in Bihar (Rs. 220.7) and the highest in Maharashtra (Rs. 468.5). The percentage of State income devoted to education is lowest in Orissa (1.5) and highest in Kerala (3.6). Illiteracy, both among men and women, is lowest in Kerala (450 and 611 respectively per 1,000 of population), and highest in Jammu and Kashmir (830 and 957 respectively). At the lower primary stage, the enrolment of boys and girls is highest in Kerala (115.4 per cent and 100 per cent respectively of the corresponding age-group) and lowest in Rajasthan (64.0 per cent and 16.3 per cent respectively).At the higher primary stage,Kerala again stands first (67.7 and 49.1 per cent respectively for boys and girls).while Orissa comes last (16.1 percent for boys and 2.0 per cent for girls). At the secondary stage,Assam is first for the enrolment of boys(25.5 per cent) and Kerala first for the enrolment of girls (12.6 per cent).But in both respects, Orissa stands last (7.5 per cent for boys and 0.7 per cent for girls).In higher education,West Bengal stands first with an enrolment of 40 per 10,000 of population and Orissa comes last,with an enrolment of 8 only.

Education of Girls

The significance of the education of girls cannot be overemphasized. For full development of our human resources, the improvement of homes, and for moulding the character of children during the most impressionable years of infancy, the education of women is of even greater importance than that of men. As stated earlier, the education of women can assist greatly in reducing the fertility rate.

In the modern world, the role of the woman goes much beyond the home and the bringing up of children. She is now adopting a career of her own and sharing equally with man the responsibility for the development of society in all its aspects. This is the direction in which we shall have to move. In the struggle for freedom, Indian women fought side by side with men. This equal partnership will have to continue in the fight against hunger, poverty, ignorance and illhealth.

Development of the Education of Girls (1950-51 to 1965-66).

There has been a phenomenal development in the education of women-one of the most distinctive characteristics of life in modern India-in the last 150 years At the beginning of the nineteenth century, there was hardly any provision for the formal education of girls. Even at the opening of the present century, not much progress had been made. In 1901, the percentage of literacy amongst women was only 0.8. The number of girls enrolled for every 100 boys was only 12 at the primary stage and 4 at the secondary. The total enrolment in higher education was only 264 (which included 76 girls reading in medical colleges and 11 in colleges of education). Much faster progress was made in the next 50 years, both in raising their social status and in developing their education; and the progress in the last fifteen years has been almost phenomenal.

Some interesting points emerge from this data. The rate of expansion of education of girls is much faster than that among the boys so that the gap between them is gradually and steadily narrowing. At the lower primary stage, the number of girls enrolled per 100 boys has increased from 12 in 1901 to 39 in 1950 and to 55 in 1965.

At the secondary stage, the corresponding figures are 4 in 1901, 15 in 1950 and 26 in 1965. In higher education, their enrolment has increased from a mere 264 in 1901 to 40,000 in 1950 and to 240,000 in 1965. Education in mixed schools is being accepted more at the lower primary stage where 85 per cent of the girls enrolled are in mixed schools and at the higher primary stage where the proportion is 78 per cent. But there is still a considerable resistance to it at the secondary stage where only 40 per cent of the girls enrolled are in mixed schools. These resistances, however, soften down to some extent at the university stage.

Recommendations

The problem of women's education has in recent years been examined by a number of committees: the National Committee on the Education of Women under the chairmanship of Smt. Durgabai Deshmukh; the Committee on Differentiation of Curricula between Boys and Girls under the chairmanship of Smt. Hansa Mehta; and the Committee under the chairmanship of Shri M. Bhaktavatsalam which studied the problem in the six States where the education of girls is less developed.

According to the Commission, the strategy for the development of the education of girls and women will have to take two forms.

The first is to emphasize the 'special' programmes recommended by the National Committee on Women's Education; and the second is to give attention to the education of girls at all stages and in all sectors as an integral part of the general programmes for the expansion and improvement of education. With regard to the first, the Commission recommend that, as suggested by the National Committee, action should be taken on the following lines:

(1) The education of women should be regarded as a major programme in education for some years to come and a bold and determined effort should be made to face the difficulties involved and to close the existing gap between the education of men and women in as short a time as possible;

(2) Special schemes should be prepared for this purpose and the funds required for them should be provided on a priority basis; and

(3) Both at the Centre and in the States, there should be a special machinery to look after the education of girls and women. it should bring together officials and non-officials in the planning and implementation of programmes for women's education.

These special programmes, by their very nature, are temporary and will have to be pursued only till the gap between the education of boys and girls is almost bridged. But they should not be made an excuse for neglecting the second aspect of the strategy, viz., giving adequate attention to the education of girls at all stages and in all sectors. In fact, if this had been done right from the beginning, the need for special programmes would hardly have arisen. in the Commission's opinion, a stage has now been reached when intensive effort should be made to develop this aspect of the strategy so that the need for special programmes will disappear in the course of a few years.

The role of women outside the home has become an important feature of the social and economic life of the country and in the years to come, this will assume large proportions affecting a majority of women. it will, therefore, be necessary to pay adequate attention to the problems of training and employment of women.

(1) An important problem is to enable women to carry out their dual role of home-making and following a suitable career. The Census of 1961 shows that there are at present more than a million young women, below the age of 24 and with a minimum qualification of matriculation, who are working only as housewives-and this number will increase still further in the days ahead. To enable these women to participate in programmes of national reconstruction, opportunities for part-time employment will have to be greatly increased. In addition, they will have to be drawn, wherever possible, into all types of nation-building activities on an honorary basis as well.

(2) Side by side, opportunities for full-time employment will also have to be expanded. As the age of marriage continues to rise, full-time employment will have to be provided for almost all young unmarried women. it may also be expected that, as in other countries, once their children reach a school-going age, women will have a great deal of time on their hands and will desire to spend it usefully by taking up full-time employment. This need also will have to be satisfactorily met. Teaching, nursing and social service are well-recognized areas where women can have a useful role to play. Opportunities for women will have to be largely expanded in these fields and several new avenues, covering almost all the different walks of life, will have to opened out.

Education for Scheduled Tribes

It is necessary to pay special attention to the education of children from the backward classes which include the Scheduled Castes, the Scheduled Tribes, denotified communities and a few nomadic and semi-nomadic groups.

(1) In so far as the Scheduled Castes are concerned, the problem has become a little easier because of the diminution in the rigour of untouchability. For its early solution, however, the Commission recommend that the existing programmes for the education of the Scheduled Castes should continue and be expanded.

(2) With regard to the last category, it may be stated that there are several nomadic and semi-nomadic groups in the country whose educational needs have been hitherto neglected almost completely. It will not be easy to provide educational facilities for such groups. To the extent possible, such groups have to be assisted in developing more settled ways of living. This calls for a degree of fundamental reorganization in their economy and their way of life and, therefore, for close study of their problems with a view to evolving solutions which will meet their needs and secure their cooperation. While such a process of change would only be carried out over several years, efforts have to be made to provide marketing, credit, health and educational facilities in a mobile form wherever there are sizable nomadic groups. Similar facilities are required for communities which migrate from their homes for several months in the year.

(3) The problem of denotified communities is small in magnitude, but extremely difficult. Patient work over years is needed. Provision of hostels where the children from these communities can live and grow up in a proper atmosphere is probably the best solution in the long run.

Tribal people generally live in forest areas which are difficult of access and where conditions of life can be very trying. Some of them live in small concentrations in the midst of a non-tribal population; but the larger proportion of tribal people live in areas which are predominantly inhabited by the tribals themselves. Examples of these are groups of districts in Madhya Pradesh, Bihar, Orissa, the hill districts of Assam and other areas in the North-Eastern region.

The problem is comparatively simple in the former case where the tribals live in 'small pockets' or they are mixed up as it were with the rest of the population and constitute a smaller part. In such cases, special attention will have to be paid to the needs of the tribals to ensure that they receive a fair share of the benefits of educational development. But the situation becomes uniquely challenging in the predominantly tribal areas because here is presented an ideal opportunity for an integrated development. In all these areas, three tasks stand out above all others. These are, firstly, development of communications; secondly, transformation of the present system of shifting cultivation into a developing agricultural economy, including care of forests, improved systems of shifting cultivation, settled cultivation and pasture; and thirdly, development of a system of education related to the scheme of economic and social development and responsive to the cultural and economic needs of the people.

The problems of education among the tribals have received a good deal of attention in recent years. They were examined in detail by the Commission on Scheduled Areas and Scheduled Tribes under the chairmanship of Shri U. N. Dhebar. They were also discussed in two seminars organized by the Planning Commission in New Delhi and by the NCERT at Udaipur.

Primary Education

Intensive efforts will have to be made among the tribal people to provide five years' effective education for all children by 1975-76. This will need an intensive programme of parental education. Special encouragement should be given to the education of girls and this will not be difficult because women have a good status in tribal life. The teachers should be invariably conversant with the tribal languages.

The medium of education in the first two years of the school should be the tribal language and books should be specially prepared in these languages (using the script of the regional language) for use at this stage. during this period, the children should be given oral instruction in the regional language and their familiarity and command over it should be improved. By the third year, the regional language should be the medium of education. There will be no difficulty in this because the children will already have learnt the script and become familiar with the language.

It is necessary to improve the provision of educational facilities which are often very meagre. In very sparsely populated areas, Ashram Schools will have to be established in large numbers. To attract children to schools and to hold them, the working and programmes of the schools should be made to harmonize with the environment.

Vacations and holidays should coincide with agricultural and forest operations and social festivities. The school hours should be fixed to suit the work the children are required to do for their families. These measures are needed for the rural population as a whole. But they are of special significance for tribal education. Moreover, the introduction of work experience and an emphasis on art education would attract the tribal children as would the teaching of folk songs, stories and riddles which are so popular with the tribal. Tribal games and archery as well as tribal music and dances should be introduced as extra-curricular activities.

Secondary Education

Far greater attention will have to be paid, as stated earlier, to the development of higher primary and secondary education among the tribals. For this a programme of hostels is very essential. Brighter children should be picked up at the lower primary stage and admitted to hostels. Careful arrangements should also be made for giving personal guidance and some extra tuition to these children so that they will be able to perform better in comparison with the non-tribal students.

Tribal children find difficulties in getting admission to good higher primary or secondary schools. The Education Departments would have to make special efforts to secure such admission and, if necessary, offer some inducements to the schools for this purpose. Where admission to such schools requires a better preparation on the part of the students, special measures should be taken to provide this coaching to tribal students and to bring them up to the required standard. As stated earlier, tribals are fond of vocational courses. Special efforts should, therefore, be made to place them in good vocational schools, the junior technical schools, the industrial training institutes, polytechnics, etc. Special vocational schools should also be organized for the grown-up children who leave school at the end of the lower primary stage.

Higher Education

It is necessary to streamline the administration of the scholarships programme instituted by the Government of India. In this context, the Commission make the following recommendations:

(1) The administration of scholarships and other aids needs to be decentralized a great deal. Heads of institutions should be authorized to grant

scholarships, along with admission, on their own authority. For this purpose, the necessary amount should be placed at their disposal well in advance of the academic year. This could be done on the basis of the previous year's expenditure with a margin for increase.

(2) The scope of the programme should be expanded to include, not only the provision of funds but also the provision of such additional coaching facilities as may be required, watching of progress, planning ahead of careers and ensuring placement in appropriate institutions, or in other words to provide for a personal follow-up. The staff necessary for this purpose should be made available.

(3) The scope of scholarships should cover all courses available to secondary school leavers; and special preference should be given to vocational and technical courses, including those at industrial training institutes.

The basic issue in the development of tribal life and education is the provision of leadership of the right type. For the next few years at any rate, this leadership will have to come from the non-tribal people-officials and non-officials-but the ultimate solution of the problem requires the development of a proper leadership among the tribals themselves. The Commission's attempt in this field should directed to both these objectives.

There are not many non-tribal persons who want to live and work among the tribals. But a few individuals and institutions are devoted to this cause. They should be encouraged and provided with necessary funds so that they could recruit and train batches of young persons who would be willing to adopt the service of the tribals as their mission in life. Among the officials, the main difficulty is that of continuous transfers. No officer remains long enough in the tribal areas to understand their problems and to be able to identify himself with the tribal interests. Many of them are not even aware of the tribal language. In several tribal areas, the Commission found a lack of rapport between the officials and the tribal people which probably was a major reason for the inadequate implementation of developmental schemes. To overcome this difficulty, it is necessary to have sub-cadres amongst officers in all departments. The persons in these sub-cadres will be selected for their competence and aptitude for work among the tribals. Once an officer is recruited to this cadre, his work should be watched for an year or two in the first instance and if it is found satisfactory, he should be retained in it for a period of 10 to 15 years at least and posted to work with the tribals. There should be special allowances or privileges to go with the cadre which should be attractive enough for the better type of officers to compete for admission to it. Such special cadres are very necessary for teachers.

To develop leadership among the tribal people themselves, some unorthodox approaches are necessary. It is but natural that young tribals who have received secondary or higher education should go out of their areas in search of employment. The work among the tribal areas would, therefore, have to be done,for some years to come, by tribals who have received comparatively less formal education but whose identification with their people would be deeper and greater. it is necessary to pick up such young persons, give them training through specially organized courses and use them as our workers for tribal uplift. In doing so, several of the formal rules of recruitment will have to be set aside. But probably this is the only way in which some tangible progress can be made in the immediate future.

Different tribal people are at varying stages of economic and cultural development. There is much difference in the skills they have attained and in the technology they employ. Therefore, in predominantly tribal areas, each group and the area in which it lives, should be studied closely, and appropriate patterns of development worked out in close cooperation with the people. It is in terms of such a design of development that educational programmes, institutions and priorities should be proposed. A uniform approach as between different tribal areas, applied in a mechanical manner, will not secure the purpose in view.

To be able to do justice to the tasks and problems of tribal education, it is important that the Ministry of Education at the Centre and the Departments of Education in those States which have sizable tribal populations, should be equipped with special sections or units whose task it would be to study the needs of the tribal people and assist in developing educational systems best calculated to promote their welfare and development. These sections or units should work in close collaboration with other Ministries or Departments involved in the programme. Aspects of tribal education which might call for special attention will vary from area to area, and no pains should be spared in understanidng the problems which arise in different contexts.

7

Enrolment and Manpower Planning

One of the major programmes in national reconstruction is the development of our human resources, and in this there can be no limit to the education to be provided. But in any given society and at a given time, the decisions regarding the type, quantity and quality of educational facilities depend partly upon the resources available and partly upon the social and political philosophy of the people. Poor and traditional societies are unable to develop even a programme of universal primary education. But rich and industrialized societies provide universal secondary education and expanding and broad-based programmes of higher and adult education. Feudal and aristocratic societies emphasize education for a few. But democratic and socialistic societies emphasize mass education and equalization of educational opportunities. The principal problem to be faced in the development of human resources, therefore, is precisely this: How can available resources be best deployed to secure the most beneficial form of educational development? How much education, of what type or level of quality, should society strive to provide and for whom?

India has committed herself to the creation of a democratic and socialistic pattern of society. The fundamental principles that should guide the provision of facilities at the different stages and sectors of education, therefore, may be stated as follows:

— to provide effective general education of not less than seven years' duration to every child, on a free and compulsory basis, and to expand lower secondary education on as large a scale as possible;

— to provide higher secondary and university education to those who are willing and qualified to receive such education, consistent with the demands for trained manpower and the need to maintain essential standards; and to provide adequate financial assistance to those who are economically handicapped;

— to emphasize the development of professional, technical and vocational education and to prepare skilled personnel needed for the development of agriculture and industry;

— to identify talent and to help it grow to its full potential;

— to liquidate mass illiteracy and to provide an adequate programme of adult and continuing education; and

— to strive continuously to equalize educational opportunities, beginning with the elimination of at least some of the more glaring inequalities.

Increasing the Educational Level of Citizens

In the next two decades the highest priority must be given to programmes aimed at raising the educational level of the average citizen. Such programmes are essential on grounds of social justice, for making democracy viable and for improving the productivity of the average worker in agriculture and industry. The most crucial of these programmes is to provide, as directed by

Article 45 of the Constitution, free and compulsory education of good quality to all children up to the age of 14 years. In view of the immense human and physical resources needed, however, the implementation of this programme will have to be phased over a period of time. This can be done

— by providing five years of effective education to all children by 1975-76 and seven years of such education by 1985-86;

— by making part-time education for about one year compulsory for all children in the age-group, 11-14 who have not completed the lower primary stage and are not attending schools. The aim will be to make these children functionally literate and stop all further additions to the ranks of adult non-literates, and

— by efforts to liquidate adult illiteracy.

The second and the third programmes are transitional. But the first needs great emphasis as the only permanent solution of the problem.

Provision of Secondary and Higher Education

Several complex problems relating to the amount, type and quality of education to be provided arise in respect of secondary and higher education. It is not easy to determine the size of total enrollments in the absence of clear and precise targets about overall expansion rates. Moreover, as education at these stages has to be diversified into a large number of courses to meet varied individual aptitudes as well as social requirements for trained manpower it becomes even more difficult to decide the precise extent of provisions for each course. Unfortunately, an understanding of these problems is still limited. Enrolment policy must, therefore, be based on a pragmatic combination of four different criteria: the public demand for such education; the full development of the natural pool of ability; the capacity of the society to provide the educational facilities needed at given levels of quality; and manpower needs for national development.

Public Demand for Secondary and Higher Education

During recent years, the demand for secondary and higher education has increased enormously. There are several reasons for this, such as:

— the traditional social status attached to a university degree;

— the growing hunger for education among the urban people and the middle classes who have realized that the best, and probably the only worthwhile legacy they can leave to their children, is to give them good education;

— the awakening among the rural people and the lower classes who are now seeking social advancement-just as the urban and middle classes did during the last hundred years-through education and government service;

— the disappearance of the old values' attached to primary education which makes secondary education the 'minimum' and higher education the 'optimum' qualification for any worthwhile job;

— the absence of adequate employment opportunities for young persons so that many of them are forced to go in for secondary or university education simply because they have nothing else to do;

— the increasing provision which is being made by State Governments for free secondary education and for the liberal grant of free studentships, stipends and scholarships at the university stage; and

— a rapid multiplication of educational institutions at this level which has made them easily accessible to young persons in thousands of small and out-of-the-way places.

This situation could have been met in two ways, either by expanding facilities in secondary and higher education strictly on the basis of available real resources in terms of teachers and materials and adopting a policy of selective admissions to bridge the gap between the public demand for such education and the facilities actually provided, or by adopting a policy of open-door access and providing all the resources needed to create the required facilities and to maintain them at the optimum level of efficiency. But as it was neither possible to resist the demand nor to raise all the needed resources, a compromise approach was attempted: the access to all secondary education was provided on an open-door basis; and in higher education, both the selective and open-door policies were operated upon simultaneously in different sectors.

This policy has had several undesirable consequences. As overall resources were limited and were absorbed in programmes of expansion of general education, it became impossible to pay adequate attention to programmes of qualitative improvement or vocationalization. Most of this expansion has also been non-egalitarian since secondary schools and colleges enrolled students who had access to them and who could afford the expenditure involved, although their preparation and motivation were often inadequate. On the other hand, they failed to enrol a large proportion of talented students who were prevented from studying further by social or economic handicaps. The benefits of expansion thus went largely to the privileged rather than to the under-privileged classes. Moreover, there grew up an imbalance between the development of general and vocational education, the former far exceeding demand

and the latter generally falling much below it. Consequently, the output of matriculates and of graduates in arts and commerce was in excess of demand and created problems of educated unemployment while trained personnel for the development of agriculture, industry or research remained in short supply.

During the next two decades, the demand for secondary and higher education will increase still further as primary education becomes universal and the general economic conditions improve. Under these circumstances, a continuation of the earlier enrolment policies will merely accentuate these evils. It is, therefore, necessary to adopt some definite policy of 'selective admissions' so as to relate enrolments to facilities available and to maintain standards.

Abilities

Providing secondary and higher education to all the potentially able students generally sets up a very high target which even affluent societies find it difficult to achieve. It will be obviously beyond our reach, at least in the immediate future, in view of the limited resources available. This should, however, be the goal towards which we should continually move. In the transitional period, immediate effect should be given to one important implication of this policy, viz., to ensure that all gifted students, who complete primary or secondary education are enabled to study further in institutions of secondary (or higher) education.

Capacity to Provide Facilities

In planning enrolment facilities, it is essential to take into consideration the real resources available and the capacity of the society to create the educational facilities needed or in demand. There are internal constraints in every educational system which limit expansion of facilities, especially in secondary and higher education. These are the availability of competent teachers, of physical plant and of finance. Even in affluent societies, these built-in constraints make it almost impossible to provide all those facilities, quantitatively and qualitatively, which would be required on the basis of public demand or for the development of the total pool of ability. This is all the more so in a developing economy like our own. In trying to meet the pressures of the public demand, these constraints are often overcome by diluting standards. There are many instances where institutions have been started without the necessary teachers being available, without the needed equipment and without adequate financial allocations. This all too common practice must be resisted in the larger interests of the country. If a society does not have the resources to meet the entire public demand for secondary and higher education, that is really unfortunate; but it would be tragic if this limitation was ignored and educational standards were thrown in jeopardy.

Manpower Needs

If India is to achieve its targets of economic growth it must have an adequate supply of educated specialists for each category of job to be performed. Conversely, if there is an excess of trained people in any category, it implies an imprudent use of scarce resources and also creates difficult problems of unemployment of the educated. Even from the point of view of the individual, some matching of educational patterns and job opportunities is vital. Nothing is more frustrating than to be underqualified or overqualified for a job, or to be unemployed because there is no call for one's qualifications. The Commission believe, therefore, that estimates of future manpower needs form a useful basis for regulating enrolment patterns above the primary level.

This broad recommendation of relating the provision of educational facilities in secondary and higher education to estimated manpower needs has to be understood in the light of some general reservations. Manpower forecasting is not a precise operation because of the large number of imponderables involved. It is, therefore, necessary to make a continuous effort to improve the collection of necessary data and the techniques of forecasting. This should be done regularly by the Central and State Governments.

As manpower forecasts are ordinarily expressed in quantitative terms, the expansion of educational facilities tends to receive undue emphasis in translating them into enrolment terms. It is, therefore, essential to emphasize the quality of manpower produced because economic growth can be hindered rather' than accelerated if appropriate standards are not maintained. Moreover, manpower needs cannot be the only criterion for regulating the provision of facilities.

Before final decisions are taken, its indications will have to be checked with the conclusions drawn from calculations based on the other criteria. However, even after making due allowance for these limitations, estimated manpower needs provide four broad indications in terms of magnitudes, e.g., the total enrolments needed in secondary and higher education; enrolments needed in different types of courses; shortages and surpluses in the manpower situation; and priorities involved.

Strategy of Development

It will be seen from the foregoing discussion that the minimum level of expansion is provided. by the capacity to expand facilities in terms of real resources and that the public demand for secondary and higher education as well as the need to develop the available pool of talent to the fullest extent possible generally set high targets which are difficult to realize in the immediate future. The gap between these high and low targets can be bridged by considerations which emerge from manpower needs and equalization of educational opportunities. These will indicate the priorities to be adopted, the different courses of study to be developed, the extent to which facilities should be provided in the different courses and the manner in which enrolments in them could be made to include at least the best students in the community.

Forecast of Manpower Needs

The Kothari Commission have recommended that educational facilities at the post-primary stage should be broadly related to manpower needs. The Commission have been fortunate in having two estimates prepared for us: one, a series of elaborate investigations carried out by the Institute of Applied Manpower Research; and the other, a part of a longer study undertaken by the Planning Unit of the Indian Statistical Institute, New Delhi, and the Unit for Economic and Statistical Studies on Higher Education,

London School of Economics, in collaboration with the Perspective Planning Division of the Planning Commission. In broad orders of magnitude, the results of the two estimates are similar; and the differences between them can generally be explained by the different assumptions used. For the main presentation of this chapter,the Commission adopt the ISI-LSE estimates as they are more detailed, offer estimates up to 1986 and assume a higher target of economic growth. The Commission believe that the risk involved in over-estimation is comparatively less than in under-estimation and that it is less harmful to have some surplus trained personnel on hand for some time rather than hold up the progress of agriculture or industry for lack of such personnel. At any rate, precise figures are less important than broad directions of policy. On this, both estimates largely agree.

Broadly there were 5.2 million workers with qualifications equivalent to matriculation and above, two-thirds of them in towns and the rest in rural areas. Over half of these were employed in 'other' services (public administration, education and so on). About one in five of them (1.1 million) were also graduates, and these were even more heavily concentrated in the service occupations. Only some 100,000 were in manufacturing industries.

The question we must ask is how these numbers may be required to grow in the future. How many matriculate and graduate workers should there be in 1976 and 1986 ? Two broad methods have been used to answer these questions, one for services, in which many educated people are employed, and one for the other sectors of the economy.

To take the latter first, it has been assumed that, as net output in each sector and in each branch of manufacturing industries increases, so proportionately will be the employment of educated manpower. The targets for economic growth assumed in these estimates, for the economy as a whole and for each sector, are those proposed by the Perspective Planning Division of the Planning Commission. The overall growth targets are 6.6 per cent a year from 1961 to 1976 and 7.0 per cent for the whole period of 1961 to 1986. Within these overall targets, sectoral targets naturally vary-from 11.85 per cent (factory establishments including power supply) and 11.24 per cent (construction) to 3.86 per cent (agriculture) in the period 1961-76. Projecting the growth of output in each separately allows for shifts in patterns of employment and reveals demands for educated workers in fast-growing highly technical industries which would be lost in a simple overall growth rate.

Within services, each major service has been treated separately. In 1961, a quarter of employed matriculates and a similar proportion of employed graduates were in public administration and defence.

On the other hand the proportion of those completing class VII who go on to be matriculates and graduates must fall. This is because of the very substantial expansion of numbers in class VII as the Constitutional Directive on free and compulsory education is implemented. If the transition proportions remain fixed even when all children complete class VII, the stocks of educated manpower would be well in excess of manpower needs. This would become especially serious from mid-1970s onwards: by 1986 there would be 4 million 'too many' matriculates and 1.5 million too many graduates.

In addition to these estimates for workers with broad educational levels, separate estimates have been made for engineers and agricultural graduates. These will be discussed elsewhere.*41 When graduates in engineering and agriculture are taken with those in medicine and teaching and related to the total stock of graduates, they form an increasing proportion-33 per cent in 1961, 43 per cent in 1976 and 46 per cent in 1986. Comparable changes are required at lower levels.

The final stage in the calculation is to say what enrolments are implied by the out-turns required. This has been done on the basis of these observed relationships between enrolments and out-turns in 1960-61, allowance being made for the Commission's recommendations on the pattern of education, length of courses, wastages, etc.

Educational Implications of Estimates

The Commission broadly accept these forecasts, subject to periodical revision, as a basis for a national enrolment policy and invite attention to the main conclusion they indicate with regard to future educational development. These are:

— to restrict the unplanned and uncontrolled expansion of general secondary and higher education, if massive educated unemployment is to be avoided;

— to make special and intensive efforts to vocationalize secondary education and to develop professional education at the university stage; and

— to devise suitable machinery, at both the national and State levels, which will relate the estimates of manpower needs effectively to the output of the educational system so that, by and large, there is some assurance that a suitably trained person would be available for every job to be done and every educated person would find a job appropriate for his education and professional training.

In order to restrict unplanned and uncontrolled expansion of secondary and higher education, it is necessary to restrict the provision for places in accordance with manpower estimates and wherever the applicants for admission exceed the places, to make the admissions on a selective basis. At the lower secondary stage, however, which is to be regarded as completion of general education, emphasis should not be laid on' selection' in the sense of admitting the 'fit' students and weeding out the 'unfit'.

At this level, selection should be oriented more towards' testing and guidance' than towards 'elimination'. Its main objective should be to enable a student to know his own level of achievement and his potentialities and to decide whether it would be in his interest to leave the school and enter the world of work, or to join a particular vocational course, or to continue in the stream of general education. In other words, selection' at this stage will be mostly 'self-selection' helped through a testing and guidance service. This service should be available to all schools in all areas, irrespective of the level of expansion of secondary education.Whether a system of more rigorous selections is needed or not in a particular area is a matter for local decision and will depend upon the needs for manpower in the area and the level of expansion already reached.

Beyond the lower secondary stage, a system of selective admissions becomes inescapable in view of the limited resources available. This idea is gaining much wider support but is still opposed on certain socio-economic grounds. It is argued, for instance, that this policy would adversely affect access to higher education of the backward classes, the rural areas and under-privileged groups now entering higher education for the first time. These fears have some Justification. But the remedy is not to be sought in the continuance of the present policy of open-door access. The under-privileged sections have a very small and disproportionate share in existing facilities in spite of the unrestricted admissions. This inequality would be removed more quickly, not by continuing the present laissezfaire policy, but by adopting positive measures to promote equalization of opportunities, such as the grant of scholarships on the 'school cluster' basis recommended elsewhere.

When such measures are provided on an adequate scale and it is clearly demonstrated that they increase the proportional enrolment of the backward or under-privileged groups in institutions of higher education, opposition to selective admissions will quickly diminish and even disappear. As a transitional measure, however, these fears may be allayed, if necessary, by adopting a suitable system of reservation of seats.

It is often argued that secondary and higher education should be given to all young persons who have completed primary and secondary education and cannot find jobs and it is further contended that such asylum for them is a lesser evil than leaving them on the streets. This is an escapist attitude, commonly observed in developing and labour-surplus societies, to over-educate young persons by regarding education as a substitute rather than as a preparation for work. In industrialized and labour deficit societies, job opportunities are so plentiful that many young persons remain in school largely because of compulsory laws.

As soon as the compulsory age-limit is reached, a large proportion (varying from 30 to 75 per cent) leave school and take up employment. This helps also in improving standards in educational institutions, because resources are plentiful in relation to the number of places to be provided in postcompulsory education. In developing and labour-surplus economies, on the other band, employment opportunities are so poor that 'opportunity costs' of education are very low and young people join secondary schools or colleges either because there is nothing else to do, or in the pious hope that a job may be more readily available from the raised platform of a higher education. But as resources are limited and the number of seats to be provided is larger, standards in secondary and higher education remain poor. The result, in some cases, is a negative rather than a positive contribution to individual and social life.

Much of the opposition to a policy of selective admissions would disappear if good methods of selection were evolved. Existing methods of selection tend to be based on a rather rigid acceptance of examination marks.

This approach finds popular support because of its apparent 'Justice', facility of administration, and because of a fear that any discretion given to individual institutions may lead to favouritism, nepotism, casteism or even corruption. But examination marks are an undependable measure of native talent or of potential growth. They are also socially unjust, being heavily weighted in favour of urban students and children from well-to-do homes and good schools. What is needed is a reliable method of selection which will take account of past performances, native talent and the principles of social justice. Educational research will have to be developed vigorously to discover such methods. Suggestions for reform of present methods are discussed later.

If enrolment in higher secondary and university education should be related to broadly determined national goals for trained manpower,. two steps are needed. The first is to fix the number of places in university departments. or colleges in advance, keeping in view the manpower needs and the facilities available; and the second is to make admissions to these places on a selective basis with due regard to the natural talents of the students, their achievements at earlier stages, and the principles of social justice.

A policy of selective admissions is already being implemented, to a large extent, in courses in science, technology, medicine and agriculture and even in a fair number of institutions of general education which are anxious to maintain standards. The techniques of selection now in force will have to be improved on the lines indicated above. Moreover, it has now become urgent to ensure that the principle of selective admissions becomes the national policy for all courses and institutions of higher education, including courses in humanities and commerce and in the affiliated colleges.

Development of Vocational Education

Estimates of manpower needs also serve as a guide for the expansion of vocational education. At the lower secondary level, leading to matriculation, we must realize that the manpower data available give little guidance on the extent of vocationalization. Manpower needs are expressed in terms of matriculates only or in terms of pupils successfully completing courses of general education. Pupils in schools for technical or industrial education, arts and crafts training, or for music, dancing and other fine arts are not represented in the manpower data. How far these courses should expand and what new courses of a vocational or practical nature should be started are questions which can be answered only after further study.

At the higher secondary level, leading to intermediate or its equivalent, considerable guidance is given by the manpower forecasts. These suggest that by 1985-86 there should be 2,413,000 enrolments in vocational schools and perhaps 600,000 in vocational colleges out of total enrolments of 6,873,000. This is equivalent to 43 per cent of the total. The Commission are of the view that vocational education at this level has to be emphasized. The Commission have, therefore, assumed that enrolments in vocational courses at this level would be about 50 per cent of the total.

At the undergraduate level, forecasts of the need for specialists suggest some 833,000 enrolments in 1985-86, in engineering, agriculture and medicine. To this must be added the enrolments in degree courses in teaching and law.

The total enrolments needed as well as the percentages of enrolments in different sectors which are derived from manpower data are not highly precise. The central principle on which they have been calculated, i.e., the Tinbergen formula, is itself open to question on several counts. The calculations are further complicated by the difficulties inherent in the available statistical data. But all things considered,the Commission believe that they do offer a broad guide to the order of magnitude involved and for the formulation of a national enrolment policy. But, as stated earlier, these will have to be continuously revised in the light of the experience gained, improved techniques discovered and availability of more refined data.

Three other points deserve notice. The first refers to financial feasibility. Forecasts of manpower needs on these lines give only a broad quantitative indication of the needed workers according to broad levels of educational attainment. But the education and training of the number of workers indicated at given levels of efficiency may require expenditure of an order which the economy will not be able to afford. It is, therefore, necessary to examine the financial implications of the manpower needs continuously. The maintenance of proper standards should always be ensured. But where the total cost of the proposals goes beyond the finances available, priorities will have to be determined and enforced.

The second is the availability of real resources to train the manpower needed. In a poor country, money is difficult to be raised, no doubt. But it is easier to raise money than to find the necessary real resources, i.e., teachers, equipment and buildings. It is much easier to create a post than to find a suitable person to hold it. In spite of funds being available, for instance, the shortage of staff in engineering institutions is of the order of 30 per cent or more.

Equipment, particularly of foreign manufacture, is in short supply; and grants for buildings remain often unutilized because steel and cement are not available. It is therefore necessary to examine the forecasts of manpower needs continuously and plan for only that level of expansion which would be feasible in terms of real resources available. While every effort should be made to increase the allocation of real resources to education, it will be dangerous to expand facilities, in the absence of real resources, by diluting standards. In a situation of this type, hard choices about priorities will have to be made.

When we think of increasing trained manpower, we should also think of the manner in which the existing trained manpower is being utilized. There is reason to believe that a fair proportion of our trained manpower is being under-utilized; and in some cases, it even remains unutilized. A continuous effort to study the problem is needed. To the extent we increase the utilization of existing trained manpower, there will be an immediate gain without further investment. It will also alter the forecasts for the future, either by reducing the numbers needed or by increasing the level of achievements.

The Commission is in full agreement with Shri Gopalaswami that there is need to correlate the development of higher education broadly with manpower needs and the Commission also agree with him in the statement of the following four objectives and implications of this policy.

First, the annual requirements of the country in respect of additions to the national stock of higher educated manpower should be assessed in advance with as much precision and firmness as may be found to be practicable. Arrangements should be made to secure that the assessed requirements are adequately met by the annual supply of higher educated manpower cohorts made available by all the higher educational institutions in the country.

Secondly, arrangements should be made to ensure that higher educated manpower cohorts will not remain unemployed or wastefully underemployed. Employment should be made available as nearly as may be possible in those capacities in which they are able to make the best use of the educational preparation given to them.

Thirdly, the courses of studies which are at present provided in higher educational institutions should be reviewed in the light of the changes which are occurring in the pattern of employment of higher educated manpower cohorts. The structure and content of these courses of studies, as well as admission requirements, should be reviewed and the entire system reformed so as to provide the best possible educational preparation for the different occupational groups of higher educated manpower.

Fourthly, there is need for developing a new type of 'promotional extension courses of studies for secondary educated persons who are already in employment and are found suitable for promotion, so as to raise their educational level to parity with that of higher educated manpower. Special arrangements necessary for this purpose should be devised and developed.

One specific proposal needs mention in this context. Pressure on higher education can be considerably reduced if the Central and State Governments were to recruit the personnel for all their services, not at the end of the first degree as is done at present, but at the end of the higher secondary stage.

Machinery for Manpower Planning

At the national level the Planning Commission has the responsibility for preparing estimates of manpower requirements in all sectors of national development and for revising them continuously. It may also consider the desirability of setting up, for this purpose, a Standing Committee for Manpower consisting of the representatives of the Ministries of Defence, Education, Food & Agriculture, Health, Home, Labour & Employment, Railways, and others concerned with the training of large and easily identifiable categories of manpower. The UGC on behalf of the universities-the largest producers of highly educated manpower-and the Institute of Applied Manpower Research should also be represented. This Committee should work in close collaboration with authorities for manpower planning at the State level. Its main responsibility should be to prepare and revise, from time to time, manpower forecasts for the overall output of the educational system as well as for different categories of specialists. These should be published for general information and for the guidance of those called upon to make decisions regarding the provision of educational facilities. The Committee should also advise Ministries of the Government of India and the State Governments on manpower problems and their implications for educational planning.

At the State level, it may be desirable to set up State Committees for Manpower on the broad lines of the Standing Committee for Manpower at the Centre and having similar functions and responsibilities. It would be a duty of the State Committees to prepare State-level plans for manpower development. Similar plans at the district level should also be prepared as soon as practicable. The universities in the State should be closely associated with this Committee. When this machinery is in place, the best possible estimates of the requirements of manpower will be available at the national and State levels, and, where necessary and possible (e.g., in respect of primary teachers), even at the district level.

The next problem is to relate these estimates to the intake and output of the educational system or, to 'plan' the facilities to be provided in educational institutions in accordance with manpower requirements. This will have to be done both at the national and at the State levels.

(1) *National Level.* Planning at the national level should be done by the Centre in consultation with the States and should cover all sectors crucial for national development, where the mobility of trained personnel is or should be high, where it is very costly to set up institutions for training personnel or where the very high level staff required for such institutions is in short supply. These should include engineering, agricultural and medical education, and the preparation of teachers for higher education.

(2) *State Level.* The planning of the remaining sectors should be done at the State level by State Governments. The universities, which train all the higher level manpower and the district educational authorities who will be in charge of all education below the university level, should be closely associated with a programme to be developed on the following lines:

(a) The planning facilities in secondary and higher education should be done at the State level.

(b) The provision of vocational education-both of school and college standard-will have to be expanded in all areas on a priority basis in keeping with the manpower needs. The same is also applicable to many areas of science education.

(c) For enrolments in general education, however, which is underdeveloped in some areas and over-developed in others, a policy of equalization will have to be adopted. Decisions will have to be made by each State in view of its conditions; but as a general basis, the following may be suggested:

(i) In all areas where the level of expansion reached is below the national average in 1966, steps should be taken to promote expansion.

(ii) In all areas where the level of expansion reached is about equal to the national average expected in 1986, a restrictive policy should be adopted unless there are special reasons to the contrary.

(iii) It will be for the Government of India to suggest the targets to be reached, from time to time, at the State level. State Governments may, in their turn, indicate suitable targets at the district levels.

(iv) The planning of higher education should be done on a State-basis. All universities in the State should be involved in this. Each university should be required to prepare a five year plan of the facilities to be provided in all its teaching departments and affiliated colleges and the output therefrom, and these should be approved after bringing them into accord with manpower needs. In granting affiliations or expanding their departments, the universities should be required to follow these plans.

(v) It is also essential to have an authority at the district level which can plan all school education. This authority will have to plan in the light of general directives given from the Centre and the States. In order to assist it in its work, local studies of manpower needs, etc., will have to be carried out.

EDUCATION AND EMPLOYMENT

In the present educational system there is no direct link between education and employment and no attempt is made even to establish an indirect link, by relating the output of the educational system closely with manpower needs or job opportunities. The recommendations made above will establish this link indirectly. But we might consider whether it would be possible to establish a direct link between education and employment.

Under a good arrangement, every graduate should be given, along with his degree or diploma, an offer of appointment as well. This offer need not be binding and it may be left open to the Student, with the approval of the Government, to accept another offer. Moreover, the period of the offer may also be made brief-one to three years-so as to avoid any undue hardship. But a compulsion on the State to make such an offer would be the surest guarantee that the output of the educational system is closely linked-with employment opportunities or manpower needs. It will also improve the motivation of the students, give a purpose to their education, and make them feel that the country needs them and is waiting for them.

In the Commission's opinion, this change could be an important factor in raising standards in higher education and in reducing the problems of discipline to the minimum. It may not be possible to do so in the present situation, when the output in some sectors far exceeds the possibilities of employment. But we should strive to move towards this goal over a period of years; and we should make at least a beginning in a few selected sectors where numbers are manageable. The system of one-year internship, which is now prescribed for medical graduates, is a good beginning in this direction, though there is a certain resentment against it at present on the ground that the medical profession is singled out for this compulsion. If the system were to become more widespread and made applicable to one category of graduates after another till all categories were covered, this resentment would disappear and the efficiency of the system would also improve.

Significant problems of life cannot be solved in isolation. The planning of education is no exception to this general rule and, in the Commission's opinion, it may not be possible to find a satisfactory solution to it unless wider issues are solved. For instance if manpower planning is to be successful in the sense that there would be a trained man available for every job to be done and that an appropriate job would be available for every educated person, it is necessary to prepare an integrated plan of development-a plan which will consist of three parts: family planning, economic development and educational reconstruction. At present, the labour force cohort (i.e. the boys and girls who attain the age of 16 or over and enter the labour force in a given year) suffers from several serious defects or difficulties such as the following:

— Its size is too large-about 2 per cent of the total population-owing to the large birth-rate.

— Its educational attainments are also very meagreabout 60 per cent of the cohort is non-literate and about 40 per cent would have completed primary schooling and attained permanent literacy. Of the latter 40 per cent, about 25 per cent would have received more than five years of schooling and probably completed the primary school course; about 8 per cent would have completed the secondary school; and only about 1 or 2 per cent might be graduates. The proportion of the educated persons in these cohorts is far too inadequate for the creation of a modern social order. What is worse, the little education that has been given is so predominantly academic that there are no trained persons to man the key posts in certain sectors of industrialization now being developed.

The rate of economic development, especially in rural areas, is so slow that there are not enough jobs for even half of this cohort. If this situation is to be improved, it is necessary to prepare an integrated plan of development with these objects:

— to reduce the birth-rate to about half in a planned programme of 10-15 years;

— to bring about a very rapid economic development in such a manpower that there would be a job for every young man or woman who enters the labour force; and

— to provide such education to the young boys and girls as will qualify them by having a specific job to do, to participate effectively in the national development programme.

Such plans are needed at the national, State and even district levels. Their preparation and implementation is the responsibility of the Government-Central, State and Local. It is only in the wider perspective of such plans that the problem of educational planning can be successfully solved.

8

Educational Planning and Administration

The crux of the problem of educational planning in India is to evolve a national policy in education in spite of the fact that education is largely a State subject in the Constitution and that a multiplicity of authorities at different levels make decisions on all aspects of the situation. This is not an easy task and as there is little similar experience to guide us, the Commission will have to evolve our own techniques in most cases. It is also necessary to review and improve our planning techniques.

A review of the first three five-year plans in the different States and at the national level highlights the need to improve the planning techniques in some directions. These have been indicated below.

(1) *Over-emphasis on enrolment and expenditure.* There has been an over-emphasis on achievement of targets in enrolments and expenditure. It is true that expansion was badly needed and that it will have to continue. But an over-emphasis on this aspect leads to the neglect of the still more important aspect of quality. Similarly, an over-emphasis on expenditure targets tends to distort priorities and often leads to wastage. There is thus a need to take a more comprehensive

view of the problem and to evolve a broader pattern of goals, especially those relating to qualitative improvement.

(2) *Need for concentration of effort and adoption of a selective approach.* Throughout the first three plans, the general policy has been to do something in every sector or for every programme with the result that the meagre resources available were spread thinly over a very large area. This policy involves considerable wastage. It has, therefore, now become important to concentrate on a few crucial programmes such as improvement of the quality of teachers, development of agricultural education, provision of good and effective primary education for all children, liquidation of illiteracy, vocationalization of secondary education, establishment of major universities, expansion and improvement of postgraduate education, increase in the number of scholarships and development of about ten per cent of institutions at each stage to optimum levels of quality.

(3) *Emphasis on programmes which need talent and hard work.* The emphasis on reaching expenditure targets to which a reference has been made tends to place a premium on programmes where it is easy to incur expenditure, e.g., construction of buildings or expansion of enrolments. This is unfortunate because there are a number of programmes which call for determined effort, organization, talent and hard work rather than large financial investment. The following are some examples of such programmes:

- production of literature in the modern Indian languages needed for their adoption as media of education at the university stage;
- educational research;

— examination reform;

— preparation of school textbooks and teaching and learning materials ;

— in-service education of teachers and officers of the Education Departments;

— improving techniques of supervision;

— improving contact with the local communities and parents;

— providing enrichment programmes and guidance to gifted students and some special assistance to retarded or backward ones.

A number of instances of this type can be cited. What is important to note is that, in the existing situation where the financial resources are limited, it is programmes of this type that need for greater emphasis than those which involve heavy financial investment.

Yet another weakness in our planning is the inadequacy of evaluation and research. Since planning is a comparatively new process and the Kothari Commission have to evolve our own techniques, it is necessary to evaluate our programme continuously and develop a strong research programme which will enable us to cut down costs and increase the effectiveness of the investment in education. But, by and large, this has not been done. Some attempts at evaluation have been made recently in the Planning Commission, viz., the COPP Teams have studied three problems two which were not of major significance. What the Kothari Commission recommend is the deep involvement of universities, professional organizations, training colleges, etc., in a periodical evaluation of all major programmes includes in the plans and in the development of a large-scale research programme on the lines recommended elsewhere.

The existing machinery for educational planning leaves much to be desire. It is not adequately staffed nor is the personnel engaged in it suitably trained. There is hardly any educational planning done at the district level. The planning cells in the offices of the Directors of Education are inadequate and staffed mostly by persons who have had no training in the field. Their work also is mostly administrative and financial and confined field. Their work also is mostly administrative and financial and confined to the compilation and reporting of educational and financial statistics.

There is need to improve the organization an methods of educational planning and for training competent personnel to staff the planning units in the Central Ministry of Education, the State Departments of Education and District School Boards, It should be possible for the Ministry of Education, in collaboration with the Asian Institute of Educational Planning, to undertake studies of educational planning in the different States and to conduct intensive courses for training the personnel involved in the process of educational planning in India. The subject is of such great significance that the UGC should also consider the possibility of setting up an Advanced Centre for Studies in Educational Planning. Administration and Finance.

Levels of Priorities

Education is essentially a responsibility of the State Governments. But it is also a national concern and in certain major sectors, decisions have to be taken at the national level. This implies the need to regard education as Centre -State partnership. On the other hand, it is necessary to remember that education which concerns every parent and every family has to be taken as close to the people as possible and that its administration can be best conducted by or in close planning has to be decentralized to the district level and still further down to the level of each institution. The process of educational planning in federal democracy like ours has thus to be the right blend of centralization, in the appropriate sectors, with a large amount of decentralization in other sectors and especially in administration. Care should, however, be taken that the parts fall coherently into the totality of a broad national plan, and all discordant features and contradictions are eliminated. For this purpose, it will be necessary to devise an effective machinery of Coordination. This the direction in which administration has to strive and planning has to grow.

One useful suggestion which can be made in this context is to adopt a system of priorities at different level- national, State and local. Programmes of national significance such as provision of good and effective primary education to every child, vocationalization of secondary education, postgraduate education and research, or education for agriculture and industry may be regarded as national priorities in the sense that the decisions regarding them would have to be taken by the Centre in consultation with the States and, once they are taken it should be obligatory on every State to implement them effectively and vigorously.

In several other matters, and these would form the bulk of the decisions to be made, a system of State-level priorities should be adopted, i.e., each State may be left to make its own best decision in view of local conditions. These would include problems such as making secondary education free of tuition fees and, in such matters, no attempt at a national uniformity need be made. In certain other matters, as for instance, in the provision of amenities in schools, and determining the type and scale of non-teacher costs, a system of local priorities may be adopted. The State Governments may create appropriate authorities at the district and school levels and leave them free to take decisions, within the powers delegated, and best suited to the local conditions. There should be not need to expect any uniformity in these matters between one district and another and even between one school and another. A system such as this which centralizes a few essential sectors at the national level would be much better than the present trend to take more and more decisions- crucial or otherwise-at the national and State levels. This Sometimes results in the curbing of local initiative and disregard of local conditions.

Redefinition of the Roles of the different Agencies Providing Education, It is necessary to redefine that role of the four different agencies which have been providing educational facilities in the country, viz., the Central Government, the State Governments, the local authorities and the voluntary organizations. Their present roles have arisen, not out of conscious planning but from historical circumstances many of which have now ceased to have any relevance. For instance, the divorce of the Central Government from education which was so conspicuous a feature of our educational system from 1921 to 1947 arose out of a political necessity, viz., the decision of the British Government to transfer education to Indian control as a part of the system of Dyarchy.

In the complex process of educational planning and implementation, the State Governments occupy a central and key position. They have to accept, for instance, full responsibility for all School education, but it is advantageous for them to discharge it in collaboration with local authorities. The day-to-day administration of schools, which should be as close to the local communities as possible, may preferably be delegated, with adequate resources, to duly constituted local authorities at the district level. In higher education, on the other hand, they will have to share the responsibilities with the universities, the UGC and the Government of India. In other words

— school education is predominantly a local-State partnership; and

— higher education is a Centre-State partnership.

In our Opinion, it is this basic principle that should guide the evolution of that delicate balance between centralization and decentralization which our planning needs.

Role of Private Enterprise

In our opinion, the future role of private enterprise in education should be broadly governed by the following principles:

(1) It is true that some forms of private enterprise have made a negative rather than a positive contribution to education. At the same time, we should recognize that private enterprise has played an important role in the development of education in modern India, that a large proportion of our good institutions are in the private sector and that it can continue to make a useful. The State should, therefore, make all possible use of the assistance contribution to the development of education in the years ahead. that can come from the private sector for the development of education.

(2) The growing educational needs of a modernizing society can only be met by the State and it would be a mistake to show any over-dependence on private enterprise which is basically uncertain. As the State has now rightly assumed full responsibility to provide all the needed educational facilities, private enterprise can only have a limited and minor role.

(3) Under the Constitution, private schools have a right to exist and if they do not seek aid or recognition from the State, there need be little or no interference with them. In fact, the Kothari Commission only

suggested compulsory registration for unrecognized schools.

(4) The position with regard to private educational institutions which seek financial support from the State is, however, different. Even now, they depend upon Government for the larger part of their expenditure; and when fees, which is their main source of income, are abolished, their dependence on public revenues would be very large.

(5) In dealing with private enterprise, problems relating to their teachers, grant-in-aid and control are very important. These have already been discussed elsewhere.

Role of Local Authorities

There are two historical traditions with regard to the role of local authorities-one of associating local authorities with education which grew up in the British Indian Provinces and the other of not associating them with education which grew up in the Indian princely States. The arguments for and against such association have been repeatedly stated and need only be mentioned here in brief.

It is generally agreed that local authorities do succeed in evoking local interest and local enthusiasm and effectively bring local knowledge to bear on the solution of problems. Their financial contribution to the support of education is not large. But it is not negligible either; and it is substantial in the case of richer municipalities like Bombay City. Their main weaknesses, however, are the harassment caused to teachers, through frequent transfers and postings, and through involvement in local factions and politics. This is the one reason why almost all teachers' associations have represented to us that the local authorities should not be placed in charge of educational institutions. This evil increases as the delegation of authority goes to lower levels, e.g., it is definitely greater when the authority is delegated to the block level than to the district level.

In the post-Independence period, two attempts have been made to redefine the role of local authorities in education and to evolve a uniform national policy. Unfortunately, these have not succeeded, partly because the two Committees which examined the problem made somewhat conflicting recommendations. The Committee set up under the chairmanship of Shri B. G. Kher rejected the British Indian view that the creation of local authorities and their association with primary education was necessary as a training ground for democratic self-government.

It was emphatically of the opinion that education should not be made a guinea-pig on the altar of democracy or decentralization and recommended that the interests of mass education should be the only criteria to decide whether authority over primary education should be delegated to the local bodies, and if so, to what extent. Although aware of the frequent maladministration of education by local bodies and particularly of the harassment which was often caused to teachers, it felt that these weaknesses could be overcome through appropriate measures and recommended that local bodies should be associated with the administration of primary education, with adequate safeguards to protect the interests of teachers, because such associations would further the cause of mass education and bring the goal of universal education near'.

Community Development, which was set up under the chairmanship of the late Shri Balwantrai Mehta to review the community development programme and its future organization. It was of the view that local interest and local initiative in the field of development would not be adequately involved unless 'a single representative and vigorous democratic institution' was created at the appropriate level 'to take charge of all aspects of development work in the rural areas' and invested with adequate powers and appropriate finances. Such a body, said the Committee, 'must not be cramped by too much control by Government or Government agencies. It must have the power to make mistakes and to learn by making mistakes, but it must also receive guidance which will help it to avoid making mistakes'. In accordance with this basic approach, the Committee recommended that strong local bodies should be created in rural areas and vested with adequate authority to administer all developmental programmes, including primary education.

The problem of integrating these two different traditions and the divergent recommendations of these two Committees became urgent when the State reorganization brought together areas from the erstwhile British Indian Provinces and the princely States. But so far it has not been possible to solve it and to evolve a uniform national policy. The present position shows a mixture of both the traditions, not infrequently, even in the same State.

In urban areas, the municipalities have been associated with education in Andhra Pradesh (Andhra area), Bihar, Gujarat (Bombay area), Madhya Pradesh (Maha Koshal area), Madras (Madras area), Maharashtra (Bombay and Vidarbha areas), Mysore 219 (Bombay and Madras areas) and Orissa (old Orissa province area). In rural areas, the panchayati raj institutions have been introduced and placed in charge of education in all States except Jammu and Kashmir, Kerala, Madhya Pradesh, Mysore, Nagaland and Punjab. The method of association is also not uniform. The municipalities are generally in charge of primary education; but they can also undertake other educational activities at their discretion. The panchayati raj institutions have been entrusted with lower primary education in some States (e.g., West Bengal); with the whole of primary education in some others (e.g., Madras); and with both primary and secondary education in two States (Andhra Pradesh and Maharashtra). Authority over education has been delegated to the block level in some States (e.g., Rajasthan and Madras); and to the district level in some others (Maharashtra). The systems of administration and grant-in-aid also show similar variations.

In our opinion, the policy in these matters will have to be decided on a pragmatic basis with reference to ultimate goals and local conditions. The close involvement of schools with their communities is a principle of great educational significance. At the same time, the difficulties caused to teachers under local authority management cannot be ignored and at least in the transitional stage, adequate safeguards would have to be provided to teachers.

Local authorities should realize their responsibilities and ensure that they help rather than hinder the cause of education. Here we are more inclined to agree with the Kher Committee that the decision to associate local authorities with the administration of education should be taken not on political but on educational grounds and that the only justification for such a decision should be a conviction that it would promote the cause of education and bring the goal of providing universal education nearer.

Similarly, local authorities should not be encouraged to think that they can claim to administer education as a matter of right and that this right will continue with them in spite of bad administration or harassment of teachers. The normal practice should be that a local authority is given the right to administer education as a privilege subject to two conditions-promoting the cause of education and good administration-and that this privilege would be withdrawn if either of these conditions is violated. there is no need to insist, as is often done at present, that a uniform policy must be adopted in all parts of the country simultaneously. It would be in the larger interests of education to adjust the experiment to local conditions and to permit each area to progress at a pace and in a manner best suited for its growth.

Recommendations. in view of these broad principles, the Kothari Commission recommended that the future role of local bodies in education may be defined as follows:

(1) As an ultimate objective it is essential that schools and their local communities should be intimately associated in the educational process. This will harness local knowledge, interest and enthusiasm for the development of education. Besides, local bodies can make a significant contribution to the total expenditure on education.

(2) It would, however, not be proper to look upon this democratic decentralization as an end in itself and to press for its universal and immediate adoption without reference to local conditions.

(3) The immediate goal in this respect-and this should be adopted immediately as a national policy in all the States-is to associate the local communities, namely village panchayats in rural areas and the municipalities in urban areas, with their local schools and to make them responsible for the provision of all non-teacher costs with the help, where necessary, of a suitable grant-in-aid from the States. The detailed proposals on this subject are discussed elsewhere.

(4) The ultimate goal to be reached is the establishment, at the district level, of a competent local education

authority which may be designated as the District School Board and which would be in charge of all education in the district below the university. level. This should also be accepted as a national policy. The jurisdiction of this authority should cover the entire area of the district with one exception, namely, the big municipalities in the district with a population of 1,00,000 or more which should preferably have a similar authority for their own areas.

(5) The transition from the immediate to the ultimate objective cannot be made in one jump but will have to proceed through a number of carefully planned stages. it cannot also be made simultaneously in all States and perhaps not even simultaneously in all the districts of a State. The difficult decisions regarding the type of local authority to be created, the level at which powers are to be delegated, the extent and nature of delegation, the powers to be retained by the State Government, the system of grant-in-aid, etc., are so complex that each State will have to decide them for itself, not even necessarily for the State as a whole, but perhaps separately for each district. While, therefore, the Centre may advise the States to move towards the ultimate objective as soon as practicable, it would be wrong to pressurize all States to adopt common policies in the matter. There is no inherent virtue in such a uniformity; and it may lead to better administration to recognize that, while the immediate and ultimate objectives may be assumed as national goals, there need be no uniformity with regard to thedetails of the transition from the immediate to the ultimate objective. These should be left for decision at the State level in view of local conditions.

(6) In all such association of the local authorities with education adequate safeguards should be provided to ensure that the teachers are not harassed and that they do not get involved in local factions and politics. Experience has shown that, for this purpose, it is necessary to vest the control over the teachers, not in the local authority, but in its Administrative Officer, to associate him closely with the District Education Officer in the discharge of this responsibility and to frame a fairly detailed system of rules and regulations to smoothen and guide the day-to-day administration.

(7) It is necessary to remember that it is not enough to decentralize the administration of education and to vest it in the local authority. The programme will not succeed unless intensive steps are taken to educate local leadership on the right lines, to provide the local authority with trained and competent officers who would have certain independence in the performance of their duties and to make the necessary resources available to the local authority to fulfil the responsibilities placed upon it. This will be a major task for the State Education Departments.

District and Municipal School Boards

The need for the establishment of local educational authorities at the district level has been pointed out already. The jurisdiction of the district school board should cover the entire area of the district with one exception, namely, the big municipalities in the district with a population of about 1,00,000 or more which should preferably have similar boards for their own areas. A district school board should consist of-

(1) Representatives of the Zila Parishad elected by itself;

(2) Representatives of the municipalities in the district elected in the prescribed manner;

(3) Educationists nominated by the State Government or elected by the Zila Parishad from out of the panel approved by the State Governments; and

(4) Ex-officio members, such as officers of education, agriculture, industries or other departments which administer vocational schools.

Persons in categories (3) and (4) should be about half of the total membership. A senior officer of the State Government (Class 1) should be the whole-time secretary of this board, which should be provided with the necessary administrative and supervisory staff.

The functions of this board would cover all school education in the district-general as well as vocational; it will directly administer all government and local authority schools within the district, and it will also remain in charge of giving grants-in-aid to all private institutions in the district in accordance with the rules framed by the State Government for the purpose.

Within the framework of the instructions given by the State Government, it should be a responsibility of the district school board to prepare plans for the development of school education within the district and it should also be the principal agency within the district to develop school education, the finances and guidance required for the purpose being provided by the State Government and the State Education Departments.

In big towns with a population of 1,00,000 or more, it would be desirable to establish municipal school boards on the above lines since these would be viable administrative units. It would also give an opportunity to the local people, who are better educated, more well-to-do and vocal, to take positive interest in developing an educational programme for their children. The composition, powers and responsibilities of these boards should be similar to those of the district school boards.

Each school board will maintain an education fund. The Zila Parishads (or municipalities) will approve the budget of the school boards. They will also raise the resources expected of them and credit them to the school board. In all day-to-day administration, the school board would be autonomous. The same relation would hold good between a municipal school board and its municipality.

The recruitment of teachers will be done by a special committee consisting of the chairman of the board, its secretary and the district education officer. The transfers should be effected by the same committee, subject to rules framed by the State Government, the general policy being to reduce transfers to the minimum and to allow teachers to develop loyalties to individual institutions. The salaries, allowances, and service conditions of teachers will be regulated by the State Governments and will be common to all the districts. These measures will provide safeguards to teachers; and the fact that all school teachers are serving together under the boards will be a further strength and an additional safeguard.

It may be advantageous, in some cases, not to burden the school boards with full administrative responsibilities all at once. In such cases, the entire administration of the schools may be left with the officers of the Department and the school board may be given powers with regard to planning and development. Additional powers may be conferred on it as it gains experience and competence.

Role of Central Government

Under the Constitution, the Central Government has been specifically vested with several educational responsibilities, and certain other responsibilities also devolve upon it as the Government of the Union. The more important of these are enumerated in the following entries of the Seventh Schedule.

The institutions known at the commencement of this Constitution as the Banaras Hindu University, the Aligarh Muslim University and the Delhi University and any other institution declared by Parliament by law to be an institution of national importance. 64. Institutions for scientific or technical education financed by the Government of India wholly or in part and declared by Parliament by law to be institutions of national importance.

Union agencies and institutions for:

(1) professional, vocational or technical training, including the training of police officers; or

(2) the promotion of special studies or research; or

(3) scientific or technical assistance in the investigation or detection of crime.

Coordination and determination of standards, in institutions for higher education or research and scientific and technical institutions.

In addition, the Government of India is also responsible for several other educational programmes which include: national planning; educational and cultural relations with other countries; participation in the work of the UN and its specialized agencies, especially UNESCO; clearing-house function of collecting and disseminating ideas and information; education in the Union Territories; propagation, development and enrichment of Hindi; preservation and promotion of national culture, including patronage to national art; special responsibilities for the cultural interests of minorities; responsibilities for the weaker sections of the people such as the Scheduled Castes and Scheduled Tribes; responsibility for promoting national integration through suitable programmes; and grant of scholarships, particularly at the university stage.

According to the Kothari Commission, education must increasingly become a national concern and the role that the Government of India should play in the development of education. For instance, apart from its role in the improvement of educational administration, the Commission have indicated several other Central responsibilities in education for

- the improvement of teacher status and teacher education;
- manpower planning in crucial sectors like agriculture, engineering, medicine, etc.;
- the development of a programme of scholarships;
- the equalization of educational opportunities with special reference to the reduction of inter-State differences and the advancement of the weaker sections of the community;
- the provision of free and compulsory education as directed by the Constitution;
- the vocationalization of secondary education;
- the improvement of standards at the education;
- the development of higher education and research with special reference to the postgraduate stage;
- the development of professional education in agriculture and industry;
- the promotion of scientific research; and
- the encouragement of educational research.

The Kothari Commission convinced that the radical reconstruction of education which it have recommended will not be possible unless (1) the Government of India provides the needed initiative, leadership and financial support and (2) educational administration, both at the Central and State levels, is adequately strengthened.

(1) With regard to the first, the Kothari Commission recommended that the Centre should play an important role in the development of educational research. It should make the good work done in one area of the country known to the other areas, through coordinating and clearing- house functions which cross-fertilize educational thinking, through periodical reviews and through conducting, or offering assistance to conduct or pilot experimental projects. There is also the need to establish, in special cases, Central institutions which can set the pace for others. It is but proper that, as in the past, the Central institutions thus established should largely be in the scientific and technical sector. But it is also necessary for the Centre to establish institutions specializing in social sciences, including pedagogical sciences and the humanities. These should be established in close association with the universities and be an integral part of the university system. Besides, the Centre can also develop education in the Union Territories, particularly in Delhi, to serve as a pace-setter for the other areas.

(2) As regards the general strengthening of the administration, the constitution of the Indian Educational Service, with the amendments proposed by us, is a step of considerable importance. It is also a Central responsibility to arrange for the in-service training of educational administrators through such programmes as the conduct of an administrative staff college for senior officers of State Educational Services. This will be discussed in some detail a little later. The Centre should scout for talent in different fields and make the services of the best people in the country available to the State Governments for advice and assistance in all matters.

Equally important is the role of the Central Government in providing financial assistance for the development of education. This assistance will take three forms:

1) Grants-in-aid made to the State Governments on account of their committed expenditure, through the quinquennial Finance Commissions;

(2) Grants-in-aid for development expenditure given for the plan as a whole, through the Planning Commission; and

(3) Expansion of the Central and the Centrally sponsored sectors.

With regard to the first, our colleague, Prof. M. V. Mathur, is of the view that it would be a great improvement if the Finance Commission could be a Standing Commission, mostly with part-time membership and a small, compact secretariat. Certain minimum percentages of the proceeds of income-tax and Central excise revenues could be guaranteed to the States and distributed on population basis. For the rest of the flow of funds from the Centre to the States, the Finance Commission should bold annual reviews and make necessary adjustments in transfer of revenues and grants-in-aid on the basis of needs and performance.

The Kothari Commission is not in favour of fragmenting education and putting one part in the concurrent and the other in the State list; education should, under any circumstances, be treated as a whole. It also do not agree with our colleagues and are of the view that in a vast country like ours, the position given to education in the Constitution is probably the best because it provides for a Central leadership of a stimulating but non-coercive character. The inclusion of education in the concurrent list may lead to undesirable centralization and greater rigidity in a situation where the greatest need is for elasticity and freedom to experiment. The Kothari

Commission convinced that there is plenty of scope, within the present constitutional arrangement to evolve a workable Centre-State partnership in education and that this has not yet been exploited to the full. The case for amending the Constitution can be made only after this scope is fully utilized and found to be inadequate. All things considered, the Kothari Commission recommended that an intensive effort be made to exploit fully the existing provisions of the Constitution for the development of education and evolution of a national educational policy. The problem may then be reviewed again after, say, ten years.

Educational Administration

The agencies at the national level concerned with the development of education are the Ministry of Education, the University Grants Commission and the National Council of Educational Research and Training (or the NCERT).

Ministry of Education

The present convention is that the post of the Secretary to the Government of India is not to be filled from the ICS or IAS pool and that it should be given to an eminent educationist who should be designated as 'Educational Adviser to the Government of India and Secretary to the Ministry of Education'. This is a healthy tradition and should continue. It is also necessary to make it clear that this is a 'selection post' and that it should not go, as a matter of routine, by promotion to the present advisory service or even to the proposed IES. This should be a tenure post, given only for six years in the first instance with an extension, in exceptional cases, for three or four years, but not renewable further. The selection should be made from amongst all persons 'available, official, nonofficial, IES, University men, etc. So much depends upon the selection of the right man for this post that no vested interest of any service should be allowed to stand in the way and, through a proper machinery for selection, the best man available in the country should be recruited on a tenure basis. The Kothari Commission mentioned that the present status of the Ministry of Education in the academic world is largely due to the fact that its Secretaries were selected in the post-Independence period from outside the services and from among eminent educationists.

It is extremely important that eminent educationists, outstanding teachers in universities and schools and leading officials from the State Education Departments should be associated with the Ministry of Education so that it can provide the needed leadership and command the confidence of the public and the teaching community. We, therefore, recommend that all the posts at the level of additional or joint secretaries and joint educational advisers should be divided into two categories:

(1) About half the posts should be filled from among the official ranks by promotion, i.e., from the present education advisory service (or the IES when it is constituted) and officers seconded from the State Education Departments.

(2) The remaining half should be filled from the ranks of eminent educationists and outstanding teachers in universities and schools. The term of each tenure should be five years to be renewable at the most for a second term.

The top-level machinery for advising the Union Minister of Education and executing his orders will consist of the Educational. Adviser and Secretary to the Government of India and all the additional and joint secretaries and joint educational advisers.

Two other functions of the Ministry of Education also need considerable strengthening and expansion.

(1) The first is the clearing-house function. The Ministry of Education has to function as a national clearing-house in education. This is necessary, not only in its own right, but also as an important aid to planning. What is needed is the collection of information on important educational topics from the State Governments, according to a well-planned schedule and its publication, with proper analysis, for the information of all concerned. These data should also be recollected periodically so that each publication serves as a benchmark. The Kothari Commission recommended that a well-staffed division should be created to perform this function on an adequate scale. It was not possible for us to go into the details of the various types of studies required. Some of these have been indicated in our Report in the appropriate context. The Commission suggested that the Ministry of Education may set up a committee to examine the issue and to prepare a programme for action.

(2) The second is the maintenance of a good statistical service which is another major responsibility of the Ministry of Education, from the point of view of educational planning, policy-making and evaluation. This service should have three main functions:

(a) to collect, publish and interpret educational data;

(b) to conduct statistical studies, investigations and surveys; and

(c) to make projections and forecasts for the future.

The existing statistical service leaves a good deal to be desired. At present, only the first function is being performed. There is so much delay in the collection, collation and publication of the data that it is almost out-of-date for the purpose of planning by the time it is published. Moreover, no worthwhile interpretation of the past data is done and the other two functions have been completely ignored. In order that these functions may be discharged properly, it is essential that the statistical section of the Ministry should be reorganized and strengthened. From this. point of view, the Kothari Commission make the following recommendations:

(a) A master plan should be prepared for the publication of educational data and for the surveys and investigations which should be conducted from time to time.

(b) The combination of the publication of routine statistics with studies of special problems is not desirable. The publication of routine annual statistics should therefore be the responsibility of a special unit as at present. But it will be desirable to create a new unit for the conduct of special surveys and investigations.

(c) To make this service more efficient, it will be desirable to introduce mechanization to the extent feasible.

(d) The statistical unit should continue its present function of providing training to the statistical staff of the State Governments and universities. However, there is need to tone up the quality and content of this training. The Ministry should also provide opportunities to its own statistical staff to receive training and periodic reorientation at training courses conducted by other expert bodies like the Indian Statistical Institute and the Central Statistical Organization.

(e) The statistical units of the State Departments of Education will have to be reorganized and strengthened likewise to enable them to perform practically the same functions as outlined above for the statistical unit of the Education Ministry.

Of the various advisory bodies of the Ministry of Education the most important is the Central Advisory Board of Education which has been functioning since 1935. The Minister for Education, Government of India, is the chairman of this Board and all the State Ministers of Education are members. The Government of India also nominates a few experts and representatives of different interests on the Board. It has also the representatives of the Planning Commission, the University Grants Commission and the Inter-University Board of India. The Kothari Commission recommended that this organization with all its standing committees be functionally strengthened.

National Council of Educational Research

The establishment of the National Council of Educational Research and Training has been a step in the right direction.

Functions

The principal function of the NCERT is extension work with the State Education Departments centering round the improvement of school education. It is uniquely suited for this function because the Union Minister for Education is its President and all State Education Ministers are its members. The objective of policy should, therefore, be to develop the NCERT as the principal technical agency functioning at the national level for the improvement of school education and operating through and in collaboration with the National Boards of School Education, State Departments of Education and their technical agencies like the State Institutes of Education.

Constitution

The Governing Body of the NCERT should have an all-India character, with a majority of non-officials. In particular, it is desirable to have at least one outstanding teacher from secondary schools and a person specializing in primary education, preferably a primary teacher.

Director and joint Director

The Kothari Commission recommended that the Council should have its own full-time Director and joint Director. At present the Secretary to the Ministry of Education is the Director of the Council and an officer of the Ministry is the joint Director. This is not an ideal arrangement, and the size and importance of the Council are such that it would be wrong to leave its leadership in the hands of part-time officers whose loyalties and commitments he elsewhere. The Council should have a whole-time Director of its own who should be an eminent educationist in the field. His status should be that of a vice-chancellor. His term of office should be five years, renewable for not more than one term. The joint Director would be needed mainly for the purposes of assisting the Director and relieving him of routine administrative matters.

Regional Colleges and CIE

The NCERT is now running four regional colleges for training of secondary school teachers. Our views on this programme have been fully discussed elsewhere. The Council is also in charge of the Central Institute of Education, Delhi. The Kothari Commission suggested that this institution should be transferred to the Delhi University; and the Commission hope that the Delhi University will establish a School of Education on the lines of our recomme-ndations and give a lead to the improvement of the programme of teacher education in the country.

Personnel

The success of the NCERT will depend upon the extent to which it is accepted by the State Education Departments and their technical wings and upon the extent to which it is able to assist them to solve their technical problems in the field. It would, therefore, be desirable that there is a considerable interchange and flow of officers from the NCERT to the State Departments and vice versa. This could be secured by inviting selected officers from the State Education Departments to work in the NCERT on tenure appointments. Arrangements should also be made with the State Governments under which officers of the NCERT could work in State Education Departments for specified periods.

As the NCERT has to play the keyrole in promoting qualitative improvements in school education, it is imperative that its campus should be developed speedily and the building programme given the highest priority. The present dispersal of departments and units in distant parts of the city is not conducive to efficient functioning.

The State Education Departments are the principal agency-to prepare and implement educational plans. Unfortunately no adequate attention has been paid so far to their development on proper lines. Their structure, designed during the British period for very limited purposes, continues to be substantially unchanged even to this date. Their procedures and programmes are still largely traditional and the outlook of their officers is, more often than not, rigid and conservative. It is true that there has been some expansion in the Education Departments.

But most of this expansion has been on traditional lines and has not implied any qualitative change in their functioning. Moreover, even this numerical expansion has not kept pace with the demands of the situation and has fallen far short of the expansion in the number of educational institutions, their enrolments, or total educational expenditure. In some States, programmes of retrenchment in the strength of the Education Departments have been carried out even when expansion of educational facilities was in full swing. The State Education Departments, as constituted at present, will not be in a position to assume responsibility for the complex and difficult programme of educational reconstruction outlined in this Report. It is, therefore, necessary to accord priority to programmes for the improvement of educational administration at the State level. Our major recommendations in this regard are given below.

Coordination

Coordination is very often an administrative bottleneck at the State level because educational programmes are spread over a number of departments at present. In most States, general education is in one department and under one Director of Education or Public Instruction. In some States, however, even general education is divided into two parts, college education and school education, and placed under different Directors.

Sometimes there are additional directorates for Sanskrit or art education. In three States the education of tribals is separated and placed under a different department. In all States, technical education is under a separate directorate and may or may not form a part of the Education Department.

Agricultural education is generally under the Department of Agriculture and medical education under the Medical and Health Services Departments. The industrial training institutes are mostly under the Department of Industries. Programmes of adult education are sometimes grouped with general education and, on other occasions, placed under the Community

Development Administration. It is obviously necessary that these different programmes of educational development should be coordinated properly and viewed as parts of a comprehensive whole.

To place all these different aspects of education under the 'umbrella' of a single department does not seem to be administratively feasible, and, for some time to come, the Kothari Commission shall have to accept the factual position that education will be administered by more than one department. It is, therefore, desirable to create, at the State level, some machinery to coordinate the programmes of all these different sectors of education and to take a unified view for purposes of planning and development. The following two measures may be considered from this point of view:

(1) *A statutory Council of Education should be created at the State level.* As separate arrangements have already been suggested for the development of higher education which is a Centre-State University partnership, the scope of this Council should be restricted to school education or all education below the university level. It should have the State Minister for Education as the chairman and its membership should include representatives of universities in the State, all directors in charge of different sectors of education and some eminent educationists. It should meet about three or four times a year and have a small secretariat of its own. Its principal functions should be to advise the State Government on all matters relating to school education, either suo motto or on points referred to it, to review educational developments in the State and to conduct evaluation of programmes from time to time through suitable agencies. This should be the most important advisory body at the State level and, if necessary, it may form standing or sub-committees

for different sectors and programmes. Its annual report, along with its recommendations, should be presented to the State legislature.

(2) It may be desirable to have, in addition, a standing committee at the officers level. It would include all State level officers in charge of different sectors of education and meet periodically under the chairmanship of the Education Secretary.

The Education Secretariat

At present the Education Secretary is generally an IAS officer, except in West Bengal, where he belongs to the Education Service. The Kothari Commission is of the opinion that the Education Secretary also, like the Educational Adviser to the Government of India, should be an educationist rather than an administrative officer. It will, therefore, be desirable to make this appointment a tenure post.

The relationship between the Education Secretary and the Director of Education has been a subject of long controversy since the issue was first highlighted by the Hartog Committee in 1928. The most common complaint is that the Education Secretariat completely dominates over the Directorate of Education and interferes even in purely technical matters. It has also been argued that the dual scrutiny of proposals that now takes place in the Directorate as well as in the Education Secretariat leads to considerable delays. The remedy most frequently suggested is that the Director of Education should be ex-officio Secretary or Additional Secretary to the Government.

The problem is difficult and there is no easy answer to all the complex relationship. Broadly speaking, the role of the Education Secretariat should be to examine educational problems from the administrative and financial points of view and in the wider context of government policies for development. It should give due weightage to the views of the Directorate in technical matters and assist the Director to function as the effective head of his department. The key to a successful relationship lies, however, in the 'personal equation' between the Director of Education and the Education Secretary; and where this has been of the right type, the results have been satisfactory.

Directorate of Education

At present the Directorates have grown big and there is not enough delegation of powers to the district level.

The time of the Director of Education therefore is so taken up with personnel administration and trivial details that he has no time for his principal responsibility of providing leadership in educational development. The Kothari Commission have, therefore, made two important proposals which will alter the entire functioning of the department:

(1) the constitution of district school boards at the district level and the transfer to them of the administration of all education below the university level (including the management of all government schools); and

(2) the strengthening of the office of the district inspector of schools so that he takes over almost all the responsibilities of the Directorate in his area.

When these changes are carried out, the directorate will be a compact and efficient organization concerned mainly with general coordination and supervision over the district education officers and district school boards. It will then be possible for them to vitalize education through a purposeful and dynamic leadership.

Administration Personnel

Administration is essentially a matter of faith and vision, bold and courageous leadership, and proper handling of human relations. The importance of securing the right type of personnel for it cannot, therefore, be overemphasized. The major weaknesses of the existing organization of the State Education Departments are largely related to personnel. These include: shortage of personnel at the higher level; lack of specialized staff; unsatisfactory remuneration and conditions of service; unsatisfactory methods of recruitment; inadequate provision of in-service education; and inadequate staffing.

The Indian Educational Service

The creation of the Indian Educational Service or IES is a step in the right direction and if organized on proper lines, such a service would help the progress of education. At the very outset, it should be noted that the character of the IES will have to be very different from the IAS or other Central Services. First, in education, administration is a service agency to teaching and research and not their master. Secondly, one cannot be a good educational administrator unless one is also a good teacher. Thirdly, there should always be a possibility for an educational administrator to come back to teaching or research and for a teacher to go over to the administrative side on a tenure assignment. In our opinion, the present proposal for the organization of the IES cuts across these sound principles of educational administration.

As proposed at present, two-thirds of the recruitment to the IES will have to be made directly by open competition. The persons selected will not generally have any experience of teaching or research and would have had no opportunity to show their competence in these fields. The remaining one-third of the posts will be filled by promotion from State services and some of these may be teachers in government schools and colleges. But the bulk of the teachers, i.e. university teachers and teachers in private schools and colleges will be barred entry within its ranks. This can only have a depressing effect upon the body of the teaching profession and ultimately on education itself. We, therefore, strongly feel that the method of recruitment to the IES should be as follows:

(1) Only one-third of the posts should be filled by direct recruitment at the level of the junior scale. Even these selected persons should not be placed in administration direct. Their first assignments, for a minimum period of two or three years, should be in teaching; and it is only after this initiation that they should be assigned to administration.

(2) The remaining two-thirds of the posts should be filled, partly by direct recruitment and partly by promotion at the level of the senior and higher scales. One-half of these posts (i.e. one-third of the total) would be filled by promotion from the State services. The remaining half should again be filled by direct recruitment-some at the level of the senior scale and others at the level of the higher scales. The agelimits for these recruitments should be suitably fixed, say, 35 and 45 years, and the applicants should have put in a minimum of service as teachers or should have distinguished themselves as research workers.

(3) Some posts in the IES should be available for being filled by tenure appointments of teachers for specified periods. In the same way, some posts in teaching and research should also be available for tenure appointments of persons from the IES.

The present proposal visualizes the encadrement of the posts of the principals of government colleges. There is also a suggestion that some posts of the principals of higher secondary schools should be encadred. There is no objection to a few posts of principals of government colleges or of higher secondary schools being encadred. In fact, it would be good to do so. But this does not require the creation of a teaching wing-the posts of these principals can be made interchangeable, as they are even at present, with some levels of inspecting officers.

But there are insuperable difficulties in the creation of a teaching wing as such which, if it is to be created at all, should include a large proportion of the teaching posts in higher education. This will not be possible because all the teaching posts in the universities and the vast bulk of the posts in the government colleges will have to be kept out of the IES. The attempt to create a teaching wing by the encadrement of a few posts of the principals of government colleges is, therefore, likely to do more harm than good by adversely affecting the morale of the teaching community as a whole. We, therefore, recommend that the idea of creating a teaching wing in the IES should be abandoned and the service should encadre only the following posts:

— all posts of Directors, Additional Directors, joint Directors, Deputy Directors, etc., District Educational Officers (and equivalent posts) in the State Education Departments (inclusive of the principals of government colleges and a few posts of headmasters of higher secondary schools);

— all gazetted advisory posts in the Ministry of Education;

— suitable posts in the NCERT;

— all gazetted posts dealing with educational programmes in other Ministries of the Government of India;

— suitable gazetted posts in the Education Departments of the Union Territories; and

— suitable posts of principals of higher secondary schools under the scheme of Central Schools.

Instead of creating a teaching wing in the IES, the Kothari Commission recommended that an adequate number of posts comparable to the higher scales of pay in the IES should be created in the universities and colleges. This is justified on educational grounds because the remuneration and status given to teachers and research workers should be at least equal, if not better, than those given to educational administrators. It will also prevent a drain of talent from teaching and research to administration.

Some thought will have to be given to languages required from the members of the IES. It is true that officers of the IES will need a much better command over the regional language than those in the IAS. But the advantages of the service would be lost to a considerable extent if every member of the IES is recruited and assigned only to the State to which he belongs. It should be a convention that only about 50 per cent of the IES officers are assigned to their own States; and there should also be the possibility of inter-State transfers (in addition to deputation to the Centre). Hence each member of the IES should be required to study and pass, within a given time after recruitment, tests in two other languages (Hindi and one modem Indian language which is not his mother tongue) at certain prescribed levels.

The changes the Commission have recommended in the organization of the IES and the corresponding improvement in the remuneration of teachers and research workers are extremely significant. If these are carried out, the IES will strengthen the administration without adversely affecting teaching or research.

The State Educational Services. At present, the State Educational Services are divided into three broad groups-Class I, Class II and others. In the reorganization of these services, the following points will have to be kept in view:

(1) There should be an adequate number of posts at higher levels, namely in Class I and Class II. The secretaries of the district school boards should be in Class I. The District Educational Inspectors should have adequate assistance from officers of Class I and Class II status.

(2) The methods of recruitment would have to be improved. A disturbing trend now seen is to push fresh recruitment to all posts on the administrative side of the State Education Departments lower and lower down the line. In one State, all fresh recruitment to all the departmental posts is done at the assistant masters' level. In such cases, a young talented graduate from the universities is not attracted to the service and all higher posts come to be gradually occupied by those who have risen from the ranks. What is needed is recruitment at three levels: assistant teachers' level; Class II level; and Class I level. There should be, as in the IES, suitable relaxation in age-limit while recruiting at higher levels.

(3) In the pre-Independence period, the main functions of the department were two: the control of educational institutions-public and private-and distribution of grant-in-aid. The entire cadre of the department consisted, therefore, of 'generalists', i.e. persons who had some initiation into education (as indicated by the B.T. or a similar degree) or had some experience of teaching. Their were a few special posts (e.g., Inspector of Audio-Visual Education), no doubt; but there was no special

training for the purpose and anyone could be appointed to the post and expected to learn his job by doing. Even inspections were 'general' in the sense the teaching of all subjects and look after all aspects of the school life. By and large, this tradition has continued to this day. But it has outlived its utility. With the enlargement of the functions of the Education Departments and the heavy responsibilities it has now come to assume for the improvement of education, the need for specialized officers has increased. For instance, curricular reform has assumed great significance; and yet there is not one specialist in curriculum in all the State Education Departments. Similar observations could also be made about other fields of education such as evaluation, textbooks, etc. One of the major reforms now needed is to reorganize the State Education Departments where necessary, on the basis of specialized functionaries and, what is even more urgent and important, to make adequate arrangements for their specialized training with the help of the universities. These specialist officers will be appointed at two levels-at the directorate and on the district staff.

(4) There are several anomalies in the salaries of departmental staff in the States and Union Territories. Two of these deserve notice:

   (i) Should the scales of pay in the administrative wing of the Education Department be the same as in its teaching wing or should they be different ? At present, three practices are in vogue. In some States, they are identical; in some, the scales of pay on the teaching side are kept higher, while in others, it is the other way round. The ideal position would be to keep the scales of pay identical but to add allowances either to the teaching or to the administrative side, to make up for the inconveniences, losses or disadvantages, such allowances being payable only so long as the person occupies the post. Such a system would make for easier transferability between the two wings and promote traffic both ways.

(ii) The scales of pay of the departmental staff (Class I and II) are made comparable, not with the UGC scales of pay, but with those of similar posts in other departments. This creates difficulties for the transfer of persons from the teaching to the administrative wing.

Training of Educational Administrators

The existing facilities and arrangements for the training of educational administrators are inadequate. Pre-service education for administrators is neither necessary nor possible. It is true that educational administration is one of the subjects taught on an optional basis in the courses of the M. Ed. degree in some training colleges and university departments of education. The number of places available in these courses is very limited. Their standard leaves a good deal to be desired because they are taught by persons who themselves have little experience of administration, because the literature available on Indian conditions and practices is very limited and because there are hardly any facilities for giving practical training to the students. Such preservice education can only be of limited use and one has largely to rely on in-service education for the training of educational administrators.,

Unfortunately, there is little or no provision for such training opportunities at present in any State Education Department. This is all the more surprising because the efficacy of training is the basic assumption in education.

Training for an educational administrator is needed, not only because the tasks he is required to perform are difficult and complex, but mainly because it is necessary to orient him to the programme of educational expansion and improvement which has to be implemented in the next two decades and to the role which educational administration should play therein. From this point of view, the Commission make the following recommendations:

(1) At the non-gazetted level, the number of officers is very large and arrangements for their in-service training would necessarily have to be made at the State level. The Kothari Commission recommend that the State Institutes of Education, in collaboration with the universities, where necessary, should organize the in-service education programmes of all the non-gazetted educational staff on the administrative and inspectional side. The objective should be to provide an in-service training of about two months to every officer in every five years of his service. In addition, they should also organize conferences, seminars, and workshops for the gazetted staff.

(2) At the level of the gazetted officers, the number in any given State is not large enough for developing a training 'institution at the State level. We, therefore, recommend that the Ministry of Education should run a National Staff College for senior educational administrators of the State Departments of Education.

(3) The task of an educational administrator is generally so heavy that he gets no time to read and to keep himself abreast of educational thought. The programmes of in-service education recommended above will correct this weakness to a great extent. In addition, it will be desirable to revive the old

practice of giving three months' leave on full pay for every five years of service, for undertaking special studies in educational problems. Preferably still, the idea of a sabbatical year of leave should be extended to senior posts in administration. He should also have the option to add to this his unutilized privilege leave (which now more or less lapses), if he desires. The only condition attached to this leave should be that the officer should submit a report on his studies at the end of the leave period.

(4) Some incentives should be provided for the officers who improve their qualifications materially through programmes of in-service education.

National Staff College for Educational Administrators

The Kothari Commission attach importance to the establishment of the National Staff College for Educational Administrators and would Eke to indicate broadly the manner in which it should function.

(1) The object of the college should be to provide in-service education, for about eight weeks, in every five years of service, to all the senior officers in the education service-IES and State Educational Services (Class I and Class II).

(2) t should have a permanent and whole-time staff of its own. In addition, it should use, as resource personnel, senior officers of the Education Departments and the Ministry of Education. As educational administration cannot function in isolation, competent persons from other departments also should be utilized for purposes of training. This will incidentally serve an important objective of such training, namely, to bring the young recruits to the cadre in living contact with senior officers.

(3) It should have a research wing where studies would be conducted in problems of educational administration. It should maintain a good library of books on the subject, both Indian and foreign. Besides, it should also function as a clearing-house of administrative procedures and practices in the States and Union Territories.

(4) As very little material on Indian conditions is available for purposes of training, the college should be established immediately and its first assignment should be to prepare a number of case studies and other data which can be utilized for conducting the training programmes. This may well take about one or two years. It is only when a thorough preparation of this type is made that the training programmes should be started.

(5) It should conduct two types of courses; a longish induction course should be provided for new recruits and shorter courses of 3-6 weeks for officers already in service.

(6) In every course conducted at the college, some officers from every State and a few from the Union Territories should be included. It should be an object of policy to cross-fertilize administrative experience.

(7) It should conduct periodical conferences, seminars and workshops on matters relating to educational administration.

(8) It should conduct a journal on educational administration and maintain a publication wing.

Increasing the Strength of the Department

The most common complaints that were placed before us by the State Education Departments were: they are understaffed; the growth in the departmental staff does not precede but follows the growth in the number of educational institutions and is never able to keep pace with it; norms fixing the number of officers required on the basis of educational institutions, teachers and students, distances involved, problems of transportation and such other relevant factors are not generally fixed and, even if fixed in theory, are not observed in practice; the expenditure for increasing the departmental staff always has a low priority and is not sanctioned automatically when programmes of expansion are approved; and the axe of retrenchment within education falls, more often than not, on the departmental staff. Most of these complaints are genuine. The Kothari Commission recommended a reversal of these policies, subject to one reservation. It is better to have a fewer officers at a higher level than a large number of officers at a lower level and on inadequate scales of pay. Our recommendations regarding the new techniques for administration and supervision provide for this; and this point should be kept in view in the proposed reorganization of the State Education Departments.

Procedures

The existing procedures in educational administration suffers from an excessive emphasis on uniformity and rigidity. In every State, the Kothari Commission heard complaints by the headmasters of government schools that almost every detail of the life of a school was regulated by the orders of the Department. The managements of private institutions also complained of rigid departmental attitudes and attempts at controlling even the smallest details. The need to change these old traditions cannot be over- emphasized.

The idea of creating uniformity and regulating the educational process through comprehensive departmental codes has been overdone and has killed all freedom and initiative and reduced experimentation to the minimum.

The Kothari Commission must now initiate a new process under which the administration win be distinguished by elasticity and dynamism.

The rule book grows bigger as the ideas grow fewer. Thus almost every well-established organization is a coral reef of procedures that were laid down to achieve some long-forgotten objective. An organization must therefore have some means of combating the process by which men become prisoners of their own procedures.

Introducing Elasticity and Dynamism

The Kothari Commission have made a number of suggestions in this regard in the earlier chapters. Here the Commission would like to emphasize some general suggestions:

(1) The first is a change in the attitude of the administrator. He should cultivate an openness of mind and a spirit of inquiry rather than a rule-of-thumb approach which tries to stick to established practices, even when they cease to be meaningful. It is here that research in educational administration and the inservice training of educational administrators can play a significant role.

(2) The second is to establish a practice of holding periodical reviews, say, every three to five years, of important administrative practices, with a view to chopping off dead wood and putting in fresh grafts, where necessary.

(3) The third is to build up,inter-State contacts and to encourage comparative studies in different State practices in all administrative matters. The study of educational administration developed in the USA out of one peculiar feature: the variety of administrative practices in the different States which arose from the fact that education was a State

subject. This variety led to a comparative study of different practices in each aspect of administration. This comparison was originally restricted to mere tabulations which showed the differences. But it soon led to a discussion about the origin of these differences, the fundamental principles on which each such practice should be based, and a comparison of the relative advantages and disadvantages of different practices. Out of this arose a science of educational administration and when the States were confronted with those comparative studies year after year, they were stimulated to think and to make innovations. This happy and fruitful crossfertilization of administrative practices has not occurred in India.

There are hardly any comparative studies it has conducted or promoted in educational administration with the result that the intellectual contact between the different State Education Departments is very little. The Kothari Commission find officers in every State Education Department who know about the USA, the UK, or the USSR, but they do not know what is happening in other States of India. If periodical comparative studies in educational administration could be prepared and the State Education Departments closely involved with them, the sad picture would soon disappear and administrative efficiency will begin to rise.

(4) An area in which there is scope for improvement in our administrative practices is that of project preparation. Modem administrative practices in both the armed forces and industry require a systematic analysis and preparation before an operation or new activity' is launched. In education, too often the practice is to describe a scheme in a page or two with some sketch of the budget required and to

begin operation with no more preparation than this. Where large sums of money are to be spent, a series of preparatory steps are all justified beginning from feasibility studies and going through to detailed, step-by-step plan of operations for the project. This detailed programming of the planned projects will ensure more economic use of resources and more detailed evaluation of the progress being made in project implementation. The evolution of this technique and the training of officers in them is the responsibility of the State Institutes of Education and the National Staff College for Educational Administrators.

(5) The traditional system of administration is based on the principle of having a few officers who are assisted by a large army of superintendents, assistants and clerks, because it was originally devised at a time when the administration had to be run by a few Englishmen with the assistance of a large number of Indians in subordinate positions. Under a system of this type, most of the work tends to be done by unimaginative persons at a lower level who were described by Burke as the 'tyrants of the desk'. This is one contributory cause to the rigidity of the system. We, therefore, recommend that the modern 'officer- oriented system' where most of the work will be done by officers at their own level with the help of a small secretariat staff should be adopted.

EDUCATION ACTS

At present the educational legislation in the country presents a motley picture: in most States, it is scattered in a number of laws and the A of it is still in the form of executive orders, the only State to have an Education Act being Kerala. We,therefore, recommend that education should be given a statutory basis everywhere and in all sectors and that an Education Act should be passed in all the States and Union Territories. This should be a comprehensive and consolidating measure which will replace all the miscellaneous laws which now exist and which will also provide a statutory basis for certain important aspects of administration which now exist merely in the form of executive orders.

The Kothari Commissionrecommended that the Government of India should issue a statement on the national policy in education which should provide guidance to the State Governments and the local authorities in preparing and implementing education plans in their areas.

9

Recommendations to Improve Educational Quality

A good deal of attention has been directed in recent years to the techniques of revitalizing classroom teaching in Indian schools. Basic education was intended to revolutionize all life and activity in the primary school and draw out 'the best in the child-body, mind and spirit'.

Considerable efforts have been made during the last decade through seminars, workshops, refresher courses and summer institutes to introduce the teacher, especially at the secondary stage, to new techniques of instruction. The use of audio-visual aids has been on the increase in urban schools, and even television has been brought into the service of classroom teaching in Delhi.

Yet it will be generally agreed that the impact of these activities on teaching practices in the vast majority of our schools has not been very significant. The picture is particularly dismal in the rural areas, and especially in the primary schools. In the average school today, instruction still conforms to a mechanical routine, continues to be dominated by the old besetting evil of verbalism and therefore remains as dull and uninspiring as before.

Why does this happen ? The problem is complex and the answers to it are not easy to give. But in the Commission's opinion, the following are the four major factors that impede progress:

(1) The weakness of the average teacher. By and large, the competence of the average teacher is poor; his general education is below standard and Ms professional preparation unsatisfactory.

(2) The failure to develop proper educational research on teaching methods. Little has been done to find out in crucial sectors the methods that are best suited to our conditions and needs. For instance, the best methods of teaching beginning reading in a phonetic script like Devanagari have yet to be developed.

(3) The rigidity of the existing educational system. Better methods of teaching are discovered, not so much through educational research, as through the adventures of gifted teachers who have the courage to get off the beaten track. Our educational system is not designed to encourage initiative, creativity and experimentation on a large scale and is, therefore, not able to keep itself abreast of the times.

(4) The failure of the administrative machinery to bring about a diffusion of new and dynamic methods of teaching. Even assuming that a good method of teaching is discovered and is actually introduced in a few progressive schools, the problem still remains of diffusing it among the other schools so that it becomes the common practice in the educational system as such. This is a difficult task, and we have yet to find the right techniques for accomplishing it.

Elasticity and Dynamism

In a modern society where the rate of change and of the growth of knowledge is very rapid, the educational system must be elastic and dynamic. It must give freedom to its basic units-the individual pupil in a school, the individual teacher among his colleagues, and the individual school (or cluster of schools) within the system to move in a direction or at a pace which is different from that of other similar units within the system without being unduly hampered by the structure of the system as a whole. In this process, the freedom of the teachers is the most vital; it is almost synonymous with the freedom of the school, for the pupils can rarely be freer than the men and women who teach them. It will, therefore, be quite in order to equate the elasticity and dynamism of an educational system basically with the freedom of teachers.

It has to be remembered that advances in classroom practice never occur on a broad front, with all the teachers and all the schools moving forward in unison. In a school system with a large number of untrained or poorly trained teachers, there is need for a solid framework of detailed syllabuses, textbooks, examinations, frequent inspections and well-defined rules.

The average teacher who wants security rather than opportunity for creativity may welcome this support. But the work of the best teachers can be crippled if they are not permitted, encouraged and helped to go beyond the departmental prescriptions. The success of an educational reform will depend upon this flexible approach where the good school or the good teacher is able to forge ahead and the necessary supports are provided to the weaker institutions to introduce the reform gradually. The task of the administrator or inspector in such a situation becomes very difficult. He cannot take the easy line of imposing common restrictions on all or be daring enough to give equal freedom to all.

One of the essential conditions for making an educational system elastic and dynamic, therefore, is for the administrator to develop this competence, to discriminate between school and school, between teacher and teacher, and to adopt a flexible mode of treatment for individuals or institutions at different levels of development. This alone can help to promote initiative, creativity and experimentation on the part of the teachers.

Certain general conditions are necessary to promote this elasticity and dynamism, some of the more important of which are given below:

(1) The individual teacher is most likely to try bold changes in teaching practice if there is a feeling of reform in the air and if he sees his small contribution as part of a major social revolution.

(2) The experimenting teacher must have much more than the passive acquiescence of the school inspectors. He must feel that officers of the Education Department are personally eager to see experimentation and that they are willing, within reasonable limits, to accept a proportion of failures as part of the price.

(3) The inspectors are the key figures in any reform of classroom practice. They are Authority, present and obvious. They should be consulted from the beginning, should know that their criticisms and suggestions carry weight, and should be made to feel that the proposed changes are, in some measure, their reforms. A school system can be no more elastic or dynamic than the inspectors will let it be. This is why the inservice education of inspecting officers assumes great significance.

(4) The sympathy and support of headmasters and senior teachers must be won quite early in the programme if they are not to dampen all youthful

ardour to experiment and explore. They may not want to break new ground themselves. But if they do not feel they are being by-passed and that the new system is not being foisted on them, they can become its patrons, if not its practitioners. There is also much to be gained by winning the approval of teachers' organizations to any movement that increases flexibility in the school system. Individuals will experiment more readily if they feel that experimentation has the general support of the profession.

(5) Anything that breaks down the isolation of the teacher increases his sense of assurance and makes it easier for him to adventure. The strengthening of the teacher's sense of inner security is a purpose common to all the methods advocated to increase the elasticity or dynamism in a school system. It is the basis of all real reform in teaching practice. There are occupations where amass advance can be achieved by the invention of new equipment and the issuing of instructions for its use. No worthwhile advance is possible in teaching method unless the individual teacher understands what he is doing and feels secure enough to take the first new steps beyond the bounds of established practice. It is easier for a teacher to do so in a small group than when he is working alone. The success of 'eam teaching' in introducing new teaching techniques into some American schools is based on the fact that it is not the individual but the team that is responsible for the planning and execution of new methods. it is our belief that the proposed organization of a school complex in which the teacher works in a cooperative group is more likely to help flexibility than the present system of isolation.

(6) Nothing reduces a teacher's sense of security or his willingness to take advantage of freedom so seriously as does his ignorance of the subject-matter he has to teach. If he is only a few lessons ahead of his class he dare take no risks, and finds safety in the old routine of rote memorizing. Increasing the teacher's level of general education is, in general, the surest way of ensuring that some of them will adopt livelier and more meaningful methods of teaching. Fortunately, the limiting factor is not so much the absolute amount of knowledge the teacher has but the gap between what he knows and what his pupils know. Consequently, the easiest place to introduce innovations is in classes I and II. There is also a great advantage in taking the lowest classes of the school as a starting point for reform, since it is at this level that the greatest 'pupil wastage' occurs through repetition and drop-out.

(7) When in doubt, teachers will teach in the way they were taught themselves and not in the way they were told to teach. So, if a school system is to become more flexible and teaching methods more lively and varied, it is essential that these qualities be established very early in the practice, as well as in the theory, of at least some of the teacher-training institutions. A few training institutions at both the primary and the secondary levels should become centres for devising, testing, and adapting methods and materials to be used in the schools.

(8) A teacher or institution will be able to introduce innovations more easily if the parents of the pupils know enough about their purpose so as not to have any fear that they will interfere with their children's chances at the final examination. A strong and respected headmaster or teacher can probably best will over the parents by his own efforts; but in most

cases, it will be necessary for the Department to help in convincing parents that changes in methods are desirable and officially approved.

(9) Innovations are more likely to occur if there is a ladder of promotion up which the bright young teacher can hope to climb by outstanding service.

(10) Obviously, elasticity or dynamism will be increased if there is a reasonable provision of books, teaching materials, and services that will enable some children to undertake part of their work alone or in groups. There is a limit to what can be expected of the most imaginative teacher if all he has is a bare room, a blackboard, a standard textbook, and sixty pupils. The most pressing needs for a teacher who wants to branch out on new methods are, therefore, a good supply of books and paper, and particularly at the lower levels of school education, some simple tools and materials for making equipment. If some teachers in the more poorly equipped schools are to have a real chance to make use of any freedom they are given, it would seem desirable to have at the disposal of the district education officer a sum of money, not too tightly bound up by regulations, that might be used, with discrimination, in providing the minimum facilities and services to certain schools and teachers who show a special willingness and capacity to adopt new methods and standards of teaching. The amount of such aid should never be so great as to make any experiment expensive, unreal, and incapable of being applied widely. Too many 'pilot projects' are conceived on such an elaborate scale that they irritate teachers in the average schools and are of little value to the system as a whole.

If measures like those described above can be taken, schools and teachers will have opportunities to venture forth on their own and try out new ideas and experiments. Of course, those that will actually utilize this freedom will be few. But it is these few teachers and schools whose work will put dynamism into the system as a whole and help in raising standards, in breaking new ground and in continually adapting the system to the demands of a changing society.

Diffusion of New Methods

Elasticity in a school system is obviously of limited value unless the good practices developed by a few adventurous teachers or schools are spread more widely through the system as a whole.

Unfortunately, this is by no means an automatic process in education, where successful experiments frequently die with the men and women who started them, and where the natural rate of spread of even the more viable innovations is measured in decades rather than in years. It takes a great deal of administrative skill and preseverance to get bold new methods understood and accepted by the body of average and below average teachers, even when they have amply proved their value and firm proofs of success are hard to produce in education.

The difficulties are multiplied ten-fold when teachers are expected to accept, not a new technique for achieving the old ends, but methods that embody in themselves a new concept of the very purpose of education. That is why it is such a long and burdensome task to convert a school system based primarily on memorization into one involving understanding, active thinking, creativity and what has come to be called 'problem solving'. Each step is not a step but a leap into the unknown, and the average teacher needs skilled and detailed help, and what may seem to be a contradiction in terms sympathetic goading if he is to make it at all.

Very little systematic research has been undertaken on the diffusion of classroom practices even in the educationally advanced countries, and practically none in developing countries. The earlier researches of Paul Mort and his colleagues at Columbia University seemed to show that a period of 25 to 40 years was necessary in the United States for anything like full diffusion of a new practice, but the rapid spread of such innovations as the Physics course (which started in 1957, and is now taken by about fifty per cent of the high school pupils studying physics in the United States) has shown that, under certain conditions, the period can be greatly reduced. This experience and some others of its type seem to indicate that the educational. administrator can encourage and hasten the diffusion of new teaching practices in a number of ways, the more important of which are indicated below:

(1) Almost all the factors which render the system elastic enough for the outstanding teacher to break new ground will also make it easier for the mass of average teachers to follow his example. However, mere permissiveness on the part of the authorities will not do the trick. They will need to play a more active part, with something that comes nearer to persuasion than to pressure but which still leaves no doubt in the teachers' minds that the Education Department and its officers favour certain changes. But it must be done with sensitivity and moderation, or the teachers will come to regard the new methods as the Department's latest fad, and may try to apply them, with or without understanding, to the detriment of the normal work.

(2) The main body of teachers will accept new methods more readily if the immediate goals set before them are limited ones. This means that the methods devised by the brilliant teacher or the subject

specialist may have to be approached by stages, and that the stage demanded of each group of teachers may vary with their ability.

(3) The usual devices for in-service training such as refresher courses, workshops, demonstrations, exhibitions of work, and visits of quite long duration (days, not hours) to see the new methods at work in pioneering schools should be adopted on a large scale. Used with discrimination and skill, films, tapes or radio can bring whole lessons to quite isolated schools, though not so much for their effect on the pupils as for their usefulness in providing a model of good teaching for the teachers.

(4) Itinerant instructors, specialized in certain subjects and class-levels of techniques, and working under the general direction of the District Education Officer, are even more vital at the stage of diffusing new methods than at the earlier stage of the first experiments.

(5) Probably the quickest and most effective way of having new theories accepted is to embed them in the 'tools' of teaching-textbooks, teachers' guides, and teaching aids of all kinds. Some teaching of theory will, of course, still be essential. But it will spring from proposed practices instead of floating airily above them. The extent of the theory and the degree of detail with which the practices are set out will vary with the level of general education of the teachers. In the initial stages of development and with weaker schools, it might be necessary for teachers' guides to go into a fair amount of detail on the series of lessons to be arranged throughout the school years, the methods to be used, the teaching aids to be prepared, the activities to be encouraged, and the tests and techniques of evaluation to be employed.

The technique referred to in the preceding paragraph may be described as the laying down of 'tramlines' on which the average teacher can move forward with confidence in his teaching. This method is different from the traditional practice wider which the teacher is given lectures on general principles and is then expected to apply them with no more aid than is given by a mediocre textbook that often clashes with the very principles that are being advocated. It is, ofcourse, the administrator's responsibility to ensure that, while providing 'tramlines' for the mass of the teachers, there is still enough freedom left for the bold few to travel more freely. But with this precaution, there is no doubt that these 'tramlines' of progress are the techniques that will be particularly effective for diffusing new methods.

It is obvious that this laying down of tramlines is not a 'once and for all time' business-it requires continuous renewal. When an administrator lays down a set of tramlines with immense effort, he generally finds that his 'progressive' tramlines have become a new 'orthodoxy' and that he will have to start laying them down once again and that there will be the same old resistance for breaking away from the earlier tramlines. But that is an inevitable and perennial problem that every educational reformer must face. The provisions made to enable the outstanding teachers to leave the tramlines will help the rest also to leave them in course of nine, while the more adventurous teachers will go still further ahead to fresh fields and pastures new.

It will be seen that the essence of the Commission's recommendation is that only an elastic and dynamic system of education can provide the needed conditions to encourage initiative, experimentation and creativity among teachers and thereby Lay the foundations of educational progress. The risks of freedom and trust in teachers that are implied in this approach are not greater than those of undue restriction and distrust and they are more worth taking. We should learn to delegate authority, to trust our teachers, to encourage the capacity for leadership amongst them, to treat every institution as having a personality of its own which it should try to develop in an atmosphere of freedom. This would need dynamic leadership at all levels, determined to give education a new deal and to make every teacher, educational officer and administrator put in the best of himself in this great cooperative endeavour.

VALUE OF THE TEXTBOOK

The value of the textbook as an effective tool of learning and of diffusion of improved teaching methods has been indicated in the preceding section. A good textbook, written by a qualified and competent specialist in the subject, and produced with due regard to quality of printing, illustrations and general get-up, stimulates the pupil's interest and helps the teacher considerably in his work.

The provision of quality textbooks, and other teaching and learning materials, can thus be an effective programme for raising standards. The need to emphasize it is all the greater because it requires only a relatively small investment of resources. Moreover, a quality book need not cost appreciably more than the one that is indifferently produced.

Quality of Textbooks

Unfortunately, textbook writing and production have not received the attention they deserve. In most school subjects, there is a proliferation of low quality, sub-standard and badly produced books, particularly in the regional languages. This has been due to a number of factors among which mention may be made of

- — the lack of interest shown by top-ranking scholars so that the writing of textbooks has been generally undertaken by persons whose abilities are far from equal to the task;
- — the malpractices in the selection and prescription of textbooks which defy control;
- — the unscrupulous tactics adopted by several publishers;
- — the lack of research in the preparation and production of textbooks; and
- — the almost total disregard by private publishers of the need to bring out ancillary books, such as teachers' guides to accompany textbooks.

State Production of Textbooks

As education began to spread, the textbook industry became one of the very profitable fields for investment and the evils of the type mentioned above became more and more conspicuous. The attention of State Governments was soon drawn to them and it was decided that, in order to eliminate them, the State Governments should take over the production of textbooks.

At present, most State Governments have adopted this policy and taken over the production of textbooks. The extent to which this responsibility has been assumed shows considerable variations-some States have produced only a few books at the primary stage while others have produced all books till the end of the secondary stage. In one or two States, not only production but even distribution and sale of textbooks have been taken over by the State.

There have been some definite gains from this policy. Private profiteering has disappeared and prices have been kept low. The malpractices and intrigues which used to be so common a feature of what used to be called the 'textbook racket' have also disappeared. The quality of books has improved in several instances, although the general level of the books still remains poor and their standard does not often come up to that some of the well-established and efficient publishers.

The main reason for this failure is that the Education Departments which have taken over the responsibility of textbook production have not adequately organized themselves for it. It is this weakness that is largely responsible for the shortcomings one often sees in the State-produced textbooks, viz., failure to revise books for long periods, misprints, poor production, failure to supply books in time, etc.

The Commission highlights two points: the first is that these weaknesses do not lead to the conclusion, as some interested parties are ever eager to show, that State-production of textbooks is wrong; and the second is to emphasize the urgency for the Education Departments to organize themselves properly for this great educational responsibility they have undertaken.

State-production of textbooks, it must be noted, is only one step in the direction of improving the quality of textbooks. But by itself, it can achieve little and if adequate steps are not taken in time to organize the activity on right lines, it may even put the clock back. We, therefore, recommended that emphasis should be placed on developing the programme of textbook production on right lines. Some concrete suggestions from this point of view are made in the paragraphs that follow.

Programme at the National Level

It is essential that the best talent available in the country should be brought together to produce the textbooks and other literature needed, both at the school and at the university stages. This can only be done at the national level by agencies set up by the Government of India.

(1) For the university stage, the Ministry of Education is bringing out a series of low-priced and subsidized books in collaboration with appropriate authorities in the USA, the USSR and the UK. This is a useful scheme and its significance has now become even greater. It should be expanded and vigorously developed, along with schemes for books written by Indian authors. The Kothari Commission lay great emphasis on the latter schemes. The Commission recommended that as a matter of national policy, nearly all books at the undergraduate stage, including those for professional subjects, should be written by Indian authors. In the preparation of these books, fullest use should, of course, be made of foreign sources. This goal should be capable of realization within 5 to 10 years.

(2) At the school stage, The Commission welcome the steps taken by the NCERT to produce textbooks with the help of scholars available in the country. Some books have already come out; and more will come out soon. These books are meant for use by State Governments who can use them with or without changes. The Commission hope that the State Governments will make full use of this pioneer venture to improve the quality of their books.

(3) The production of textbooks and allied materials at the national level will be greatly facilitated if the Government of India were to establish, in the public sector, an autonomous organization, functioning on commercial lines, for the production of textbooks. The Commission have recommended the establishment of similar organizations at the State

level also. But there will be a large number of books, especially in the scientific and technical sector, which can only be produced on a national basis. It would also be desirable to produce several other categories of books at the national level, either for reducing cost or for improving quality or for purposes of national integration. We, therefore, feel that an organization of this type at the national level is urgently needed. The Commission recommended that the Ministry of Education should set up a small committee to work out the details of this project and take all the necessary steps to bring it into existence as early as possible.

Textbooks produced at the national level will have other advantages as well. One of the Commission's major recommendations is that we should make an attempt to evolve national standards at the end of the primary, lower secondary and the higher secondary stages. The definition of these standards as well as the organization of a programme for their practical implementation will be greatly facilitated by the production. of textbooks at the national level.

Such books can indicate the expected standard of attainment far more precisely than any curricula or syllabi; and their practical use in schools is the surest method to raise standards and make the teaching in schools in the different parts of the country fairly comparable. In a subject like mathematics or science, for instance, there is not much scope for local variations and the adoption of common textbooks in all parts of the country is not only feasible, but also desirable from several points of view. The same can be said about a common textbook in citizenship prepared from the point of view of national integration and used in all schools of the country. History is another difficult subject to teach, especially from the point of view of social and national integration; and authoritative well-written books on the subject can be of immense help to all teachers.

At present, there is hardly any common book which all the students in India read; and that is one of the reasons why our educational system contributes so little to national integration. On the other hand, if we had, say, a set of 100 books on different topics written by the best of our scholars which would be translated and be available in every school and if an average student were expected to read them in his school course as a matter of routine, the entire thinking of the rising generation would be different and national integration could be immensely strengthened.

Programme at the State Level

While attempts to improve textbooks at the national level are thus welcome, they cannot be the sole attempts for this crucial reform. Their most effective service is to stimulate other centres into activity and especially to promote similar enterprise at State levels.The Commission recommended that each State should organize an adequately manned expert section for the production of textbooks for schools. They should make as much use of the work done at the national level as possible. But there is no escape from the fact that each State will have to produce several textbooks in areas where national books will not be available. Even in areas where national books are available, independent attempts by the States will stimulate each other and the Centre itself. The Commission call hope for the best results only when the national and all the State centres for textbook production are functioning actively and in close collaboration.

The following points should be kept in view by the State Education Departments in organizing their programmes of textbook production:

(1) A separate agency, preferably functioning on an autonomous and commercial basis, should be set up, in close liaison with the Education Department for the production of textbooks and teaching aids. would be extremely difficult, if not impossible, to have within four walls of usual departmental procedures, the autonomy freedom which such an undertaking essentially needs.

(2) Production of textbooks is a continuous process. For instance, it takes a year or even more to produce a textbook and a further year for try-out and revision. Within a year of its adoption on a large scale, a process of evaluation has to start; and very soon thereafter, it will be discovered that it needs revision. Thc machinery set up, therefore, should be adequate to follow all these steps for every textbook. It should be an objective of policy to see that a textbook is continuously revised and kept up date and that a thorough revision takes place at least once in. five years, if not oftener. The need for frequent revisions of textbooks is obvious, even if the curricula were to remain unchanged.

(3) No useful purpose is served by having only one textbook in a subject for a given class-this is almost invariably the position under the existing programmes of nationalization. It should be an important objective of policy to have at least three or four books in each subject for each class and leave it open to the teachers to choose the book best suited to the school. This is necessary even if there were to be a common syllabus for all the schools. The Commission have recommended, however, that there should be more than one approved syllabus and that each school should be permitted to adopt the syllabus best suited to its own conditions. In

such a case, a multiple choice of books should be available for each syllabus.

(4) When Government gets books written, the payment to authors is often so niggardly that the ablest scholars are not generally attracted. This is the one point where private enterprise often scores over Stateproduced textbooks. It is, therefore, necessary to adopt liberal policies for remuneration, comparable to those of the private trade, and to attract the best people to write books.

(5) State-production of textbooks is not to be used for purposes of earning profits; its sole purpose is to produce the best books and to make them available to the children at the lowest cost. The entire organization should, therefore, be run on a no-profit and no-loss basis. The sale of State-Produced books, however, are so large and certain, that even where no profit as such is charged and the price is merely rounded off to the nearest five paise, large margins are left over and — are enough to cover the costs of research, overhead establishment and the preparation of ancillary aids like teachers' guides.

(6) The incentive to write books should be encouraged in as many quarters as possible. Apart from commissioning selected persons to write textbooks, which will have to be done in many cases, the Departments should also invite manuscripts, proposals, etc., and be ever on the hunt for new talent. There should be high level committees of professional persons to Judge books or proposals submitted; and approved books should be adopted by the Departments and published after making suitable arrangements with the authors.

(7) Special encouragement should be given to teachers to write textbooks. In the USSR, even the highest

positions in universities can be obtained by writing outstanding textbooks. Our universities can follow this example. The Commission also suggest that learned societies should give adequate professional recognition to outstanding textbooks.

(8) Good textbooks are not enough; they should be supplemented by teachers' guides and other instructional material. A teachers' guide, should give detailed assistance to teachers. Even for graduate teachers in the United States, some of the new courses being evolved in mathematics, science and social studies contain a great deal of detailed suggestions. The poorly educated and insecure teacher tends to drop into a dreary routine in which every lesson is taught in the same way, and he needs quite detailed suggestions on a variety of methods, which can make his teaching more lively and effective. It is only with the help of such detailed framework of support and guidance that a large number of teachers, particularly in the primary schools, will get off the beaten track.

There are really three aspects to the textbook production programme:

(1) Academic aspect which includes the preparation of textbooks, try-out and evaluation;

(2) Production aspect which includes all matters relating to printing and publication; and

(3) Distribution aspect which includes storage, sales, etc. The first is the most important aspect, and the responsibility for it will have to be squarely accepted by the State Education Departments. The second is discretionary. The Commission find that some State Governments have accepted direct responsibility for it and established separate textbook presses. The

third is really self-contained and is not inseparably linked with the first two. In one State where the State Government had assumed direct responsibility for distribution of textbooks, the Commission found that the precious time of a number of field officers was taken up by sales, accounts and stock-keeping. The Commission recommended that this activity should be promoted through student cooperatives which every educational institution or group of educational institutions should be encouraged to establish, and that it should not be assumed directly by the Education Departments.

Provision of Essential Teaching Aids

In assessing the needs of the teacher from the point of view of teaching methods, one is forced to admit that in the majority of schools, particularly at the primary stage, there is still an almost total absence of basic equipment and teaching aids-a good blackboard, a small library essential maps and charts, simple science apparatus, and necessary display materials. The supply of such basic equipment and teaching aids to every school in the country is essential for the improvement of the quality of teaching. It would indeed bring about an educational revolution in the country. The Commission recommended that lists of minimum teaching aids and equipment needed by each category of schools should be prepared. These may be kept as economical and frugal as possible. But once a certain minimum equipment is considered necessary, Steps should be taken to see that it is given to every school on a high priority basis. As in Madras State, the help of the local community could be harnessed in developing this programme. As a first step, the Commission recommended that a good blackboard should be immediately given to all schools.

The Commission recommended that Education Departments should work with the All India Radio for the use of radio lessons, supplemented with printed material for the teachers, and, if possible, for the pupils. The Commission also recommended the broadcasting of special radio talks, in the early morning or late evening, specially designed for teachers which will help to deepen their subject knowledge and guide them in lesson preparation. The more sophisticated forms of the newer techniques, however, can be used, generally speaking, at this stage of our educational development only on an experimental basis and in a few schools. It has to be remembered that schools cannot use an equipment which is much beyond the level of technology in the society. Sophisticated equipment given to rural schools, for instance, cannot be maintained and soon falls into disrepair. A few progressive schools may be equipped with new aids like language laboratories and programmed instructional material; but such techniques may preferably be tried out, in the first instance, in the education and training of teachers.

The majority of teachers in our schools will have to rely on inexpensive teaching equipment which are easily available in the locality or are made by them with proper encouragement and little financial assistance. The programmes that will help us most, in the immediate future, in improving the teaching in our schools are, therefore, the following:

(1) The training of teachers in the use and preparation of simple and improvised teaching aids;

(2) The use of the school workshop-and also of programmes of work-experience-to prepare the teaching aids required by the school itself and by other schools in the neighbourhood;

(3) Manufacture of simple equipment on a large scale for reducing cost, and its distribution to schools; and

(4) Sharing the more costly equipment in common by schools in a given neighbourhood. For instance, a group of schools in the neighbourhood may have a projector in common. A good laboratory in one school can be used, according to a carefully prepared plan, by other schools nearby. A group of schools may have a circulating library, and so on.

Class Size

It will be generally agreed that there cannot be a marked improvement in methods of teaching if the teacher is required to teach very large classes as a matter of routine. The phenomenal expansion of primary and secondary education in recent years has resulted in overcrowding in schools, especially in urban areas, where accommodation is not easily available for the extension of the school building or the opening of new sections. The class size sometimes grows to abnormal proportions.

A class of sixty children is a common sight in a city. The Commission ourselves have seen, in the course of our tour, classes of sixty and even sixty-five children in a few secondary schools. Quite often, the classroom is not able to accommodate easily such a large number. The problem is solved by pushing the teacher's chair-there is no place for a teacher's desk-into a corner and bringing the front benches almost up to the black-board! In conditions like these all talk of creative teaching ceases to have any significance.

Difficulties of Teaching Large Classes

Methods of teaching in classes of fifty pupils and more cannot be satisfactory. However capable a teacher may be, he cannot pay individual attention to a large number of children, give special assistance to the weaker ones, guide the brighter ones to proceed at a faster pace in an attempt to help one and all to reach the maximum of their capacities. In these circumstances the average teacher will be tempted to resort to rote memorization. Assignments given will generally not be checked and composition exercises will be marked during periods of spasmodic energy. The poor quality of teaching in the ordinary secondary school in urban areas may partly be attributed to overcrowded classrooms.

We do not, however, support those educational theorists who contend that a class should not have more than twenty or twenty-five pupils. It would be extremely unrealistic for our teachers to think in terms of this ideal. There is indeed no such thing as an ideal class size, and there is no sanctity about the number twenty-five or twenty. In our country, classes of a somewhat larger size than what may be strictly considered as desirable cannot be avoided for a long time to come. Some of the educationally advanced countries are also facing a similar problem.

Teachers should reconcile themselves to the acceptance of this inescapable necessity. It is also the responsibility of the training institutions to have a more practical approach to the problem and to evolve methods which would help the teachers to teach classes of this size without a complete abandonment of all pedagogic principles.

Fixing the Maximum Class Size

However, beyond a certain number, it is not possible to extend the class size without doing serious damage to the quality of teaching. This is particularly true at the high school and higher secondary school stages, where individual differences become more marked, requiring special help to be given in many more cases, and where the assignments to be attended to increase in number. The Commission is re of the opinion that it is not enough to fix the average pupil-teacher ratio at the different stages of school education. Such a ratio is necessary, of course, to determine the number of teachers required with reference to the enrolments. But it will not necessarily control the class size. We may have a ratio of 40 pupils to one teacher at the primary stage and yet find a class of 10 pupils and another of 80 pupils perhaps in the same district. It is essential that, in addition to the pupil-teacher ratio, the maximum number of pupils to be admitted in a class must also be prescribed, and this maximum should not be allowed to be exceeded in any case.

School Buildings

The provision of school buildings is extremely unsatisfactory at present. At the primary stage, only about 30 per cent of the schools are stated to have been housed in satisfactory buildings. The corresponding proportion at the secondary stage is stated to be about 50. This shows the great backlog of unconstructed school buildings which has to be cleared during the next few years. In addition, buildings will have to be provided for the additional enrolment which will rise with increasing speed. The problem, therefore, has three aspects:

(1) provision of the necessary funds;

(2) reduction of the building costs to the minimum level possible; and

(3) the devising of a suitable machinery which can implement the programme expeditiously and economically.

Funds for School Buildings

The Commission recommended that the allocations for

construction of school buildings In the Central and State budgets should be increased. This is one area where the local community can make a significant contribution. Schemes of grant-inaid should, therefore, be devised under which assistance from the State will be available to local communities, on a basis of equalization, for the construction of school buildings. Wherever possible, loan programmes for the construction of buildings should be encouraged. Grant-in-aid and loans should also be available to private schools, on a fairly liberal basis, for building construction.

Reduction of Costs

A number of committees have examined this question for both the Central and State Governments, on behalf of the Ministry of Education, the Ministry of Works and the Planning Commission. In addition, the UGC has prepared detailed norms for hostels, staff quarters, libraries, etc., and the Central Building Research Institute at Roorkee and the Indian Standards Institute have made recommendations in this area. The result of all these is that there exist, for most types of schools and colleges, space and planning norms and type plans and a good deal of sound advice that can help in reducing costs. What is required now is a mechanism that will put this information into practice.

In view of the acute shortage of traditional classical building materials and the shortage of accommodation, many schools are today operating in what are classified as 'temporary constructions' by the PWD and some even in thatched huts. The Commission found that there is a strong prejudice against such structures. In the Commission's view this prejudice against the use of 'temporary' buildings or thatched huts for school purposes is totally unjustified. Designed and constructed with a raised floor and high doors and windows with plenty of ventilation, these structures serve more than adequately as school buildings. This should riot, however, be misunderstood to imply that kacha buildings are always better. This is not so; and some kacha buildings prove costlier in the long run because of heavier costs of maintenance. What the Commission emphasized is the need to accept well-planned kacha structures as part of our system and to highlight simplicity and utility rather than ostentation in the construction of buildings.

Buildings in Rural Areas

The problem of school buildings needs to be discussed separately for urban and rural areas. In the former case, land values are high; and very often enough land is not available at all. Sophisticated structures are, therefore, necessary, even in order to keep in tune with the immediate environment. In the rural areas on the other hand, land is cheap and readily available; and sophisticated structures often look grotesque in a village atmosphere.

The Commission recommended that everything should be done to encourage local initiative and local contribution in cash, kind or labour for the erection of schools. A special device that can be of great use is that government should supply only the framework-which can be prefabricated-and the local people should be expected to rise the plinth and fill up the walls. The 'nucleus' approach recommended by the Ministry of Education will be of great help and deserves to be generally adopted.

Buildings in Urban Areas

In urban areas, the following steps should be taken for achieving economy in the construction of educational buildings:

(1) *Judicious Selection of Specifications and Local Materials.* The existing practice of playing safe by adopting conventional specifications is not conducive to economical construction. Economy can be achieved through the selection of locally available, materials, use of cheaper materials, omission altogether of certain finishes and acceptance of a lower standard of construction. In all these steps, the governing factors would, however, be the availability of materials, climatic conditions, safety of buildings and recurring costs on maintenance.

(2) *Techniques of Construction.* With careful planning and designing, even the so-called 'temporary' structures can be made to serve a better purpose than many of the rented buildings in which schools are often housed. Such structures should be built, wherever climatic and other conditions permit. If pucka buildings are absolutely necessary, an increasing reliance is needed on the improved techniques of construction such as the use of framed structures, cavity walls, pre-fabricated components, RCC frames for doors and Windows and components evolved by the Central Building Research Institute and other research organizations.

Expeditious Construction

In order to expedite the construction of school buildings, the following steps are recommended:

(1) *Rural Areas.* In rural areas ,there are no local contractors available. Contractors from urban areas generally charge higher rates when they are required to work in villages. The departmental machinery is also not adequate to reach most of the outlying villages. For the construction of village school buildings, therefore, the Commission recommended

that the agency of the local communities or village panchayats should be utilized to the fullest extent possible.

(2) *Urban Areas.* In urban areas, the Commission recommended that the local agencies like municipalities and corporations should be utilized fully for construction of school buildings. They have the necessary technical staff and can also contribute towards the cost of such buildings. If the responsibility for providing buildings for local schools is placed on municipalities and if a suitable system of grant-in-aid is devised, the progress in this sector would be accelerated.

Supervision and Standardization of School Buildings

For construction of government school buildings, to assist the voluntary organizations for the purpose, to supervise the general programme of construction of school buildings in a State, and to continually introduce improved and economic techniques, the Commission recommended the adoption of the following additional measures:

Each State should have an Educational Building Development Group, within the Public Works Department but working in close association with the Education Department, and consisting of an architect, an educationist, an administrator, a civil engineer and a cost accountant, all working on a full-time basis (with power to co-opt representatives of special technical skills). The main function of the group would be to improve the planning and construction of government school buildings but its advice should be available for private schools also. There should also be a Building Development Group working at the Centre, for effectively coordinating the working of State-level Groups.

The other functions of the Groups will be:

(a) to study building requirements in the light of new teaching techniques,

(b) to develop in cooperation with manufacturers new building techniques and specifications,

(c) to evolve functional and economic type plans for various types of educational buildings,

(d) to arrive at a correct assessment of costs of materials and labour required,

(e) to conduct field trials,

(f) to evaluate the plans, specifications and building techniques already in use, and

(g) to study methods of maximizing the use of indigenous materials.

The State Government should ensure that the recommendation of these Development Groups are followed.

(1) When the Groups in the different States are well established, the possibility of making them function within a rigid frame work of 'maximum cost per place and minimum standards' as is being successfully done in the United Kingdom, should be explored.

(2) To avoid delays in the construction of government buildings a separate unit of PWD should be set up for execution of educational buildings programmes.

(3) Formation of Educational Building Consortia. After the Educational Building Development Groups have standardized the plans and the technique of construction, the possibility should be examined of establishing Education Building Consortia to exploit fully the advantages of industrialized buildings.

(4) *Standardization*. Layouts, dimensions, specifications and methods of construction for any particular region should be standardized by the Educational Buildings Development Group mentioned above so that mass production of the different components on a factory scale can be undertaken resulting in economy as well as speed of construction. Considerable work in the field of standardization has been done by organizations like the Indian Standards Institute which could serve as a basis for further studies.

(5) *Buildings for Private Schools*. The economy measures worked out by the Educational Building Development Group in each State for reducing the cost of educational buildings should be made known to the managements of private educational institutions in the State, and the grant-in-aid given to a private management for a building should be subject to the upper cost limits worked out.

Bibliography

Census of India, *Literacy and Education Standard*, Paper 5, 1954.

Choudhuri, N., "What Ails our Elementary Education", *Secular Democracy*, Vol. VII (31, 32 and 33), pp. 1675-1681, 1976.

Gosal, G.S., "Regional Aspects of Rural Literacy in India", *Presidential Address*, Transactions of the Indian Council of Geographers, 1967.

Gough, Kathleen, "Implications of Literacy in Traditional China and India", in Goody (ed.) *Literacy in Traditional Societies*, Cambridge University Press, 1971.

Government of India, *The Report of the University Education Commission*, Vol. 1., New Delhi : Ministry of Education, 1970.

Kothari, R., *Footsteps into the Future*, New York, The Free Press, 1974.

—————— ., *Dossier of International Foundation for Development Alternatives*, Nyon, No. 52, 1986.

NCERT, "Education and National Development", *Report of' the Education Commission*, New Delhi, 1964-66.

NIEPA, "Womens Education in India: The Regional Dimension", 1983.

Nuna, S.C., "Inequity in Indian Education: Male-Female", *Workshop on Indicators of Equity*, NIEPA, New Delhi, October, 1983.

—————— ., "Inequity in Indian Education: Rural-Urban", *Workshop on Indicators of Equity*, NIEPA, New Delhi, October, 1983.

—————— ., "Educational Statistics in India: A Need for Appraisal", *Progressive Educational Herald*, Vol. 1, No. 2, pp. 82-86, 1987.

—————— ., "Education and Development", *NIEPA*, New Delhi, 1987.

Nurullah, S. and J.P. Naik, "A Students History of Education in India", New Delhi: Macmillan & Co., 1974.

Perulekar, R.V., *Literacy in India*, Macmillan, 1939.

Premi, Kusum K., "Educational Opportunities for the Scheduled Castes : Role of Protective Discrimination in Equalisation", *Economic and Political Weekly*, IX, 45 & 46, November 9, 1984.

Premi, M. K. "Educational Planning in India", New Delhi : Sterling, 1972.

Rao, T.S., "Free Education for All", *Social Welfare*, Vol. XIX (9), December, pp., 1972.

Raza Moonis, "Education and the Future: A Vision", *in Educational Planning: A Long Term Perspective*, New Delhi: NIEPA, 1985.

Vidyarathi, L. P. "Tribal Development in Independent India and Its Future", *Man in India*, Vol. LVI(1), pp. 172-83, 1976.

Index